# Life Hacks

*Ideas That Change Everything*

**Jon Morrison**

©2017

Life Hacks: Ideas That Change Everything

Published By: Apologetics Canada Publishing.
Abbotsford, B.C., Canada.

©2017 by Jon Morrison

All rights reserved. No part of this publication may be reproduced, stored in a retrieval system, or transmitted by any means without prior written permission of the author.

ISBN: 978-1542481267

Some names have been changed to protect identities.

Unless otherwise noted, all Scripture quotations are from The Holy Bible, English Standard Version, copyright ©2011 by Crossway Bibles, a division of Good News Publishers. Used by permission. All rights reserved.

This book is dedicated to all whom I have had the privilege of pastoring. I am convinced that there is no more humbling title that God could give someone than that of "Pastor".

*But I received mercy for this reason, that in me, as the foremost, Jesus Christ might display his perfect patience as an example to those who were to believe in him for eternal life.*
-                                                                                    1 Timothy 1:16

# ENDORSEMENTS

"Jon Morrison has written a highly accessible and practical guide to hacking some of life's most important spiritual priorities. It's filled with solid and life-tested advice that will serve you well."

>Larry Osborne
>Author and Pastor, North Coast Church

"We could all use a few life hacks, no matter what age or stage we're at, and these are gems. Jon writes with a clarity and authority beyond his years. If you practice half of what Jon talks about, you'll not only have a richer and more faithful life, you'll have a better life."

>Carey Nieuwhof, Founding and Teaching Pastor, Connexus Church; Author of *Leading Change Without Losing It*

"Jon Morrison is a rare breed; he's gifted in simplifying the big ideas of life in a way that changes how you see the world and live in it. He's the greatest life hacker I know!"

>Andy Steiger. Director of Apologetics Canada; Author of *The Thinking Series*

"I just finished reading 'Life Hacks'. My only regrets are that I didn't read this earlier in my calling as a pastor AND that I didn't think of this idea first! Jon takes his reader to a well of wisdom, reality and self-examination. I would encourage you to drink slowly and deeply. We could all use a little more grace - and Jesus offers it freely and fully."

>Grant Fishbook, Lead Teaching Pastor,
>Christ the King Community Church

Jon does it again with Life Hacks. His humour, passion for discipleship and love for Jesus are so clearly shown in this book as he seeks to guide a generation of young believers to Jesus. Life Hacks is a practical, honest and challenging read for anyone who is considering the way of Jesus.

>Chris Throness, Pastor, CA Church

Life Hacks

# TABLE OF CONTENTS

|    |                                                              | Page |
|----|--------------------------------------------------------------|------|
| 1  | Introduction: *For the Love of Hacks*                        | 9    |
| 2  | Life Hack #1: *That First Button*                            | 15   |
| 3  | Life Hack #2 - *Make Each Day Count*                         | 29   |
| 4  | Life Hack #3 - *Get Kicked Out of Cool*                      | 39   |
| 5  | Life Hack #4 - *Consider Your Calling*                       | 57   |
| 6  | Life Hack #5 - *Always Be Ready*                             | 77   |
| 7  | Life Hack #6 - *Choose Your Friends Wisely*                  | 89   |
| 8  | Life Hack #7 - *Become the Person You Would Like To Marry*   | 105  |
| 9  | Life Hack #8 - *Embrace the Desert*                          | 123  |
| 10 | Life Hack #9 - *Love the Local Church*                       | 139  |
| 11 | Conclusion: *The Life-Long Process of Life-Hacking*          | 153  |

## ACKNOWLEDGMENTS

Jesus said that everyone to whom much has been given of him, much will be required" (Luke 12:48).

I am forever grateful to the people who have invested so much of themselves into my life. Thank you to my family, mentors, pastors, friends and teachers who saw something inside this punk kid that made it worthwhile to invest time and prayer in his life. It hasn't just been people. I have also had many dollars given towards my education throughout my years at Biola University, Oxford University, and Ambrose University College. To those who supported me, you really did take a chance and I am grateful.

I want to thank my loving and supportive wife. She has read through this manuscript many times and has offered tremendous insight and help with it.

I would like to thank Joan Newton and Ginny Jaques, and Ian Hall for their work in helping with content and grammar editing. I can assure you that any remaining mistakes are my own, not theirs.

Thank you to my hard-working and talented brother for his help with the formatting of this book. You can see his work at churchos.com.

I thank Jesus for the opportunity to live, to live forever, to think and to write. I would be nothing without Jesus who gave his everything for me. This book is a token of my thanks to him.

Finally, thanks to you for taking the time to read this book. You are making all these hours of studying, wrestling, living, observing, typing and editing worthwhile.

## INTRODUCTION
# FOR THE LOVE OF HACKS

When staring down the barrel of a gun, you don't have a lot of time to process your last vocabulary lesson. An armed man wearing a balaclava was yelling something at me in Spanish but I couldn't make out one of the words he was yelling.

"Abajo! Abajo!" he was furiously shouting while pointing his gun at me.

I was lost in thought. "Abajo…I know that one..."

I was being robbed in a Costa Rican restaurant where my Latin American friends and I were celebrating the end of an amazing trip. After a month of travel, I had worked up enough Spanish to be able to stay in a conversation; however, there were still some words I was having trouble with.

"Abajo" was obviously one of them. The kids at the orphanage where I was working were fantastic teachers. They never judge you and they are as patient as anything. If you want to learn a foreign language, go to an orphanage and immerse yourself in children who speak the language. It worked for me…except for "Abajo," that is.

"Juan, get under the table!" My friend pleaded with me.

That's when I clued in. "Abajo" in Spanish meant "down" in English. The man with the gun wanted me to get down under the table. I looked around the restaurant. I was the only person not "down" at the time. I guess that's why the gun was pointed at me.

You never think that a pleasant meal with friends could turn into a heist. Life is unpredictable at times. And it is full of surprises.

Sometimes you need a helpful friend to come with you and interpret some of those surprises. I had my friend Paulo to make sense of the robber's demands. Maybe I can be yours today and help you out in some way.

That's what this book, *Life Hacks*, is about.

## What Is a Life Hack?

The Internet is mind-blowing. Granted, there is a lot of garbage out there — but the good stuff is awesome. With just a quick search, you can find almost anything you need around the globe. The Internet has helped me cook dinners, fix my car and even helped repair our beloved family stroller with a part that was designed in New Zealand, made in Asia and shipped to Canada. One of my favourite additions to the Internet is a phenomenon known as "The Hack".

A hack is something that someone discovers that makes your life just a little easier, cleaner, simpler or quicker. You can hack pretty much anything. Helpful hacks can be found on your phone, around the house, at school, or at work.

I'm a busy guy with many responsibilities at home and at work. Wanting to do more things than my schedule allows, I'm constantly frustrating myself. Life is short and, like you, I'm trying to make the most of it. To achieve this, I need every spare moment that I can squeeze out of life. That's why I need life hacks. They help us seize the precious moments of the life that God has given us.

Many hacks we can find online are helpful but short-lived. Technology is always changing. While tech hacks are helpful, they all come with an expiration date. Besides, who wants to read about a hack when you can find it on *Youtube*. But some hacks are more timeless. Those ones can and should be put into print. These are the kind that don't need to be constantly updated. That's why I'm writing about Life Hacks. These life hacks are about making your life better, simpler, richer, more efficient, and more mistake-free. Let me tell you about how I got to writing a book about Life Hacks.

## The Kid Who Needed Life Hacks

I think everybody has a box somewhere in their closet full of stuff they have collected that is too tacky to display and yet too personal to throw away. It is full of old pictures, love notes, and souvenirs from trips you can barely remember anymore. They are all kept in this special box. Every once in a while I pull out my random box and sort through it. This brings out all kinds of memories: the great ones, the funny ones and some I am still trying to forget.

Working through my own memory box, I find my grade twelve yearbook. As I go through the pages, I inevitably end up looking at my grad photo.

I pause and think about the kid in that picture. I still remember all the things that I was thinking about, worrying about, and now, with many years having passed since that day, I think about all the things about which I had no clue.

## Life Hacks

The kid in the picture had no idea about the things that were going to happen in his life. He could never have known about all the characters that would pass through his story that was still to be written. He would not have known about all the lessons he was going to learn, the successes he would enjoy and all the heartache he would both cause and endure in the coming years. I think about how great it would be to have the opportunity to take this younger version of myself out for lunch and prepare him for all that would soon come his way.

I think I could offer him some advice that would have really helped him in the years that followed. He needed some perspective on how to really savour the best days, and some wisdom on how to persevere through the difficult ones. I would have told him which phone calls to make and which calls to screen. I would have told him to read more and watch TV less. I would have told him to be more careful protecting his heart and exercise even more caution when dealing with the hearts of others. Of course, none of that is possible now. That's the reality of life.

I confess that I have found adult life to be very challenging - more difficult than I imagined when I wanted to badly to "just grow up".

In the scope of two years, I met my wife, we got engaged, got married, I did a master's degree, we bought a home…and got pregnant. Then we bought a minivan but that's for another story. Thankfully, because I had lots of time and help preparing for those two crazy years, they did not break me (though at times it felt like it would happen!). Having been through many challenges, I am so thankful for every moment, every conversation, every challenge that prepared me for adulthood.

There is so much I could tell my graduating self if I had the chance. The content of this book makes up the main points I would have covered during that chat. It is a result of the lessons I've learned since I graduated from high school. Having worked with thousands of high school grads since that day, I've become well aware of what they need to hear.

I have perceived a lack of solid mentoring and leadership and the cost that it took on our youth. In a world of a growing number of kids without parents, coaches or teachers who could be role models, it becomes even more important to provide some sort of direction for life.

There are some directions that *Google Maps* can help you with. There are other places that it cannot take you.

The thing about hacks is that we seldom discover them for ourselves. We have to be taught them. It is the same with Life Hacks.

## About this Book

You won't find the first edition of this book anywhere other than in someone's old souvenir box or perhaps at a garage sale. I wrote it in 2009 as a youth pastor as a gift to my graduating students. I had never written a book before. I saw all the terrible books that were written for grads and I didn't want to buy any of them. Instead, I wrote my first book (which was more of a really long letter for my graduating students) over a Christmas break. It was well received but needed some serious help. As the saying goes, "What is written without effort is read without pleasure." Now I've re-written the entire book (a couple of times) and received some much needed help in the process.

I would encourage you to read this book with someone else. Take time to discuss it together. You don't have to agree with everything. It's just a tool to help. That's what Life Hacks do — they help.

## One Thing Before We Begin

I don't want to assume that you really wanted to read a book today. The technology is a little dated. I understand that. Maybe you've been assigned to read this book or it was given to you by someone you love. Perhaps they gave it to you as a gift. I have been given many books by well-intentioned people. Many of them I have never read. On the other hand, I've been handed a few books that have completely changed my life. Since you've read this much already, I'd encourage you to give this book and its contents a shot. You never know what kind of a difference it could make in your life.

Whoever you are, wherever you are, I assure you that going through these next chapters together will be a lot like the puberty experience — awkward at times, challenging at others; however, in the end you will look back and be glad you went through it.

LIFE HACK #1
# THAT FIRST BUTTON

Those who teach writers how to write stress the importance of revealing some common ground with your readers early on. While I may not know you, we probably both get dressed every morning. Here's something else we have in common: we both know that you have got to get the first button on your shirt right or the whole process falls apart. If you get that first one right, the rest of the buttons will follow along nicely, and the sky is the limit for the success you might experience that day. Miss that first button and the rest of the buttons do not know what to do (and people do not know what to do with you!).

Having a relationship with God is like that first button. If you want to do your life right, you have to have a proper view of God and your relationship with him. Here's the problem with our Western culture today: too many people miss the first button entirely. As a result, their whole lives are thrown off.

## The Stuff that People Care About

Our first Life Hack is the most important. As a finite human being, I am well aware of my limitations. There are so many things that I am not good at ("so" being the understatement). I'm not good at math, home repairs, administration of any kind, and I always let my car go way too long before changing the oil (isn't that little number they put on the inside of the windshield just a recommendation anyway?).[1]

While I'm not good at many things, I do think I understand people quite well. I have been a person for as long as I can remember. Having been in some kind of ministry for more than ten years, I have met with a large number of people. I have pastored, counselled, comforted, prayed with, and taught countless souls. While we people are unique, there are many similarities between us. We have the same kinds of needs, desires, and questions. I can spot them because I have them too. I am a Christian because I believe that Christianity speaks to those needs, desires and questions better than any other worldview. It has worked for me and I have seen it work in so many lives. I have found Christianity to be both true and helpful. It is intellectually reasonable and existentially satisfying. In fact, it is so great that I have devoted my entire life to telling others this story. I want them to experience what I have experienced. I want them to know what I have learned. Knowing God is, I believe, the life hack of all life hacks.

But to get there, we need to start somewhere. Let's start with the human heart's deepest longings.

## The Philosopher's Big Four

The philosophers will tell you that the human being is a curious creature. We think about stuff and we want to understand it. We don't just want to know something in order to pass a test. We want to know something and experience it. These same philosophers will tell you that we're all going through life seeking to answer four basic questions:[2]

   1. We have questions about our origin: Where did we come from?

---

[1] It's not. I've had to learn the hard way that regular oil changes keep your car alive. Trust that little number they give you.

[2] These I have borrowed from Vince Vitale and Ravi Zacharias. They have used these four questions throughout his many years of ministry, engaging skeptics. See *Jesus Among Secular Gods* (Faith Words, New York, NY, 2017) for a fantastic treatment of these questions.

2. We have questions about meaning: What is the purpose of life? What should I be doing?
3. We have questions about morality: What is right and wrong? Should we pursue good and avoid the bad? What are the consequences for doing right or wrong?
4. We have questions about destiny: Where am I headed? What is at the end of all of this?

Imagine a place where you could get all the answers to life's big questions. What if I told you that all these questions and answers were in one book? How much would you pay to get that kind of information? How quickly would you go and get it? That book would probably be the best seller of all time.

And it is. The Bible is consistently the best selling book of the year. It has become redundant (or unpopular) to mention just how much it blows away all the other books and that's why you don't see it on the *New York Times Bestseller* list.

The Bible engages minds and touches hearts. It does this because it answers our big questions, particularly the aforementioned questions of origin, meaning, morality and destiny. It's a book that gives your life the firm foundation it needs to be firmly established.

D.L. Moody, a popular American preacher from the nineteenth-century, had the following statement written in the flyleaf of his Bible. Though its author may be unknown, its message is powerful:

> This Book contains the mind of God, the state of man, the way of salvation, the doom of sinners, and the happiness of believers. Its doctrines are holy, its precepts are binding, its histories are true, and its decisions immutable. Read it to be wise, believe it to be safe, and practice it to be holy. It contains light to direct you, food to support you, and comfort to cheer you. It is the traveler's map, the pilgrim's staff, the pilot's compass, the soldier's sword, and the Christian's charter. Christ is its subject, our good its design, and the glory of God its end. It should fill the memory, rule the heart and guide the feet. Read it slowly, frequently and prayerfully. It is given to you in life, will be open in the judgement, and be remembered forever. It

involves the highest responsibility, rewards the greatest labor, and condemns all who trifle with its holy precepts.

Those are some powerful claims about the Bible. Let me show you just how much the Bible explains the heart's biggest questions.

## 1. Origin—Where Did I Come From?

The Bible begins with the memorable line, "In the beginning God created the heavens and the Earth" (Gen. 1:1). This powerful sentence sets the tone of the whole book and creates a foundation for how we see the entire universe. "In the beginning, God created…" puts our lives in a setting in space/time history.

I realize that not everyone believes that God created the world or that God even exists. I too have had my doubts about God over the years. With each doubt, however, I go back to why I am a theist - someone who believes in God. I have written about it in another book at length so in this book I'll only give a brief explanation of why I believe that God does exist.[3]

When it comes to believing in the important things in life (like love, hope, justice, peace) we have a hard time proving they are real things. We cannot put love in a beaker over a Bunsen burner and watch it prove its existence to us. We believe in love because we have faith that it is there. Our faith in love is not blind faith. Though we cannot prove love is real, we have reasons for believing that it is. It's the same with God. No one can prove God's existence, but we can have faith in the evidence that we do have. One of my friends is an L.A. homicide detective named Jim Wallace. Jim prefers to talk about clues for God and I tend to agree with him.[4] When you take all the clues that God has given us to show that he is there, we can be certain that our faith in him is justified.

---

[3] See Jon Morrison. *Clear Minds & Dirty Feet*. (Abbotsford, B.C. Apologetics Canada Pbl., 2012).

[4] If you are interested in this idea, I recommend his books *Cold Case Christianity* (David C. Cook Publishing, 2013) or *God's Crime Scene* (David C. Cook Publishing, 2015).

I can only briefly highlight a few of the evidences I use to help others or myself to work through doubt. I believe in God because I believe science points us to God. There is a foolish idea going around Western culture these days that science and Christianity cannot co-exist. That's what I was told for years and that's what I still hear from people today. However, I believe that science and Christianity work well together.

*1. God Is the First Cause*

A major scientific discovery in the past 100 years has been an amazing confirmation of what the Bible teaches. It is also my first clue for God's existence.

The Bible says that there was a beginning to the universe and science confirmed it at the beginning of the twentieth-century with the discovery of the Big Bang. That first initial event must have had a first cause like God. Or to put it more bluntly: *Big bangs need big bangers*. It would take a being like God who exhibits the following attributes:

- Eternal. This Being had to be outside of time since it is responsible for creating time. Something or someone cannot make time if they are restricted within time.
- Spiritual. This Being must be made of a substance that is outside of physical space since it made everything that exists within our understanding of space.
- Uncaused. Whatever begins to exist has a cause. Whatever is eternal must begin all causes. For example, someone or something must be outside of the standing dominoes in order to knock the first one over.
- Immaterial. This Being had to create material in the first place.
- Personal. A choice had to be made when to begin everything. An impersonal force like the wind or gravity cannot make decisions like this. At a moment of its own choosing, a personal being must make the decision when to create everything.[5]

Who is the best candidate for all these characteristics? It is the God of the universe, the God of the Bible. In his book, Miracles, C.S. Lewis sums it

---

[5] William Lane Craig. *Reasonable Faith*. (Wheaton, ILL Crossway Books, 2008). See p.93-157.

up well, "No philosophical theory which I have yet come across is a radical improvement on the words of Genesis, that 'In the beginning God made Heaven and Earth.'"[6]

## 2. God Is the Cosmic Fine-Tuner

Science has revealed in the past decades just how finely-tuned our world is for life. Recent discoveries in all scientific disciplines cry out with astounding evidence for God's existence. Scientists are noticing design in the world and wondering aloud where this design originated. One example is from astrophysicist Dr. Paul Davies who wrote in the *International Journal of Astrobiology*, "There is now broad agreement among physicists and cosmologists that the universe is in several respects 'fine-tuned' for life".[7] Other secular scientists are clear that there is a curious order in the world. British astronomer Fred Hoyle was an atheist when he wrote the words, "A common sense interpretation of the facts suggests that a super-intellect has monkeyed with physics, as well as with chemistry and biology, and that there are no blind forces worth speaking about in nature."[8] He confessed that the evidence for God in the fine-tuning argument deeply disturbed his atheist beliefs. What was this super-intellect that had seemingly given Earth the ideal conditions to support life? This is the sort of order we'd expect to find in a universe created by a God who made the heavens and the Earth.

## 3. God Is the Information Programmer

Biologists tell us that within every one of our cells is a complex code called DNA. Bill Gates, the founder of Microsoft, has compared the genome to a computer program. Gates admits that the genome is far more complex than anything his programmers have come up with.[9] When we think of code, we think of programming by design. That's why believing in God makes the most sense here. God wrote that code. God

---

[6] C.S. Lewis, *Miracles* (New York: Touchstone, 1996), pp. 45–47.

[7] Paul Davies, "How Bio-friendly is our universe?". International Journal of Astrobiology. November, 2003.

[8] Fred Hoyle, "The Universe: Past and Present Reflections," Engineering and Science, November 1981, 12.

[9] Bill Gates, *The Road Ahead*, Penguin: London, Revised, 1996 p. 228

also explains much of the complexity we find in the cosmos, such as the order of mathematics or the precise predictability we find in the laws of physics. Such a high level of information, order and sophistication that scientists discover all the time are, to me, compelling evidences that God created the universe. When you consider the sciences, that all our discoveries are just that —discoveries— it boggles the mind to think that we never wrote the laws of math or physics, nor did we balance the periodic table. All this order and information we find in science does not come from chaos. It must come from a Super-intellect. That, to me, is God.

*4. God Is the Law-Giver*

A fourth piece of evidence for God's existence is not found through a telescope nor a microscope but within our own hearts. This is the moral argument for God's existence. Christian thinkers have long pointed out that within every person there exists a moral compass that points them towards doing what is right and avoiding what is wrong. C.S. Lewis called this the Moral Law. He argued effectively in *Mere Christianity* that if there are certain laws within our hearts then there must be a law-giver. This law-giver is God. Because I am convinced that morality is a real thing and not just a product of evolutionary survival or utilitarian philosophy, I find Lewis' reasoning sufficient evidence for God's existence.

*5. Jesus Christ Was God With Skin On*

While there are many more evidences I could give, I'm going to skip to one that I believe trumps them all. That is Jesus Christ. Jesus Christ made a bold declaration when he claimed to be God. If he was telling the truth, he is God. The logic follows that if Jesus is God then there is a God. Jesus did many miracles during his time on Earth but the greatest of them all came three days after his death when he rose from the dead.

Plenty of historical evidence supports the claim that Christians have been making for roughly two thousand years: that Jesus came back to life and is still alive today, is actually true.[10] There is no historical figure like Jesus.

---

[10] While I have written about this in my book, *Clear Minds & Dirty Feet,* I highly recommend the work of Gary Habermas, Michael Licona and William Lane Craig on this topic.

He clearly was different from everyone else. That's because he really was God.

When it comes to questions of origin, there is no case stronger than that the Creator God created this whole universe and that he created you as well. The case is strong and it is comforting. To know that my life has value and purpose— to know that I am known by such an amazing Being — that is a Life Hack worth celebrating. Knowing God as the one who made you gives life incredible meaning. That's the answer to the second question.

## 2. Meaning—Why Am I Here?

I have been writing on a personal blog since 2006. Bloggers are always trying to generate more traffic to their website so that more people will read what they are putting out there. I was recently advised that if you want lots of clicks on Google, you've got to say something about the meaning of life. Apparently, "What is the meaning of life?" is one of the most popular questions people ask Google. Google will point people to you if you can answer the question.

Answering this question is not just about getting in Google's good books. It's about our life. This is *the* million-dollar question we need to live, isn't it?

This is the question we wake up every morning wondering (perhaps only subconsciously). Many questions circle around this one: *What am I supposed to be doing today? Is my life worth living? What is the purpose of what I'm doing?* We ask these kinds of questions in classrooms, in coffee shops, and any time we go to work. What is the purpose of our being here?

Christianity, surprisingly enough (at least to many people), answers these questions. This book is designed to help you find meaning in all the areas of your life. We will talk about how to find meaning by knowing God personally, by seizing every day, by understanding your God-given calling in life, and by engaging in meaningful relationships. I wrote this book because I believe that there is a purpose for your life. You were made by God to know him and to let others know about him.

This is a Life Hack because, sadly, too many people today wake up not knowing if there is any purpose to their lives. Sadly, many people today have already ended their lives, having given up hope that their life served any purpose. Some people are showing all the signs of living a meaningful life but their worldview does not allow them to believe that their lives have meaning.

Ever since the 17th and 18th century Enlightenment, much of the West has abandoned belief in God. Without God, the answer to the meaning of life is a dark and cold echo: "You are only the accidental by-product of nature, a result of matter and time and chance. There is no reason for your existence. The only certainty is death."[11]

One of the reasons I am a Christian is because Jesus has given me a life full of meaning. It is not an easy life he offers. The journey for all of us is full of challenges. But through it all I know there is a purpose to it and a joy that comes along the way. This joy cannot always be described, it just has to be experienced.

You don't have to look to Google to find it. It's found right there in Jesus.

## 3. Morality—How Should I Live?

Morality may not be a popular word these days but moral considerations are unavoidable. Some think only right-wing religious conservatives talk about morality. This is not the case. If you ever want to see some serious preaching, buy a rusty, old, gas-guzzling SUV and keep it idling in front of a vegan art festival. Fire up some hot-dogs and lie on a bear-skin rug in front of your vehicle. Then expect lots of shouting, cussing and some hell-fire preaching because of your actions.

This is my only point: *everyone* believes in some kind of morality. It's what motivates our decisions, how we spend our money, what we endorse online and how we vote. The question really becomes: *What is your moral code and where did it come from?*

---

[11] William Lane Craig. "The Absurdity of Life Without God" http://www.reasonablefaith.org/the-absurdity-of-life-without-god#ixzz4UvIDobvz. Accessed Jan. 5, 2017.

Christians are sometimes mocked for claiming that their morality rules over all others. This is tough for a number of reasons. One, everyone thinks that their moral code is best or else they would not hold to it. Even the statement that says, "All moral claims are equal" is a moral claim. All those who hold to it expect others to hold the same position and cannot figure out why they do not. That, to me, sounds like the same superiority that Christians are accused of claiming. We must move on to the question, "*Which* morality am I going to adhere to?"

I believe Christian morality is the most humble moral code to hold. I say this because it does not come from any human. No one can say that they made it up. The Bible claims its contents are inspired by God (2 Tim. 3:16). Christians are supposed to believe what the Bible says because of its divine origin. We have the words that God inspires and the teachings of Jesus straight from his mouth.

To accept Jesus' teaching is to accept him. To accept Jesus is to accept his teaching. In Luke's gospel, Jesus is perplexed that someone might call him Lord/Master but not obey what he tells us to do. In Luke 6:46, Jesus asks rhetorically, "Why do you call me 'Lord, Lord,' and not do what I tell you?"

That's the real problem when it comes to Christianity's answer to the question, "How should I live?" We know that we should be living more in line with what God wants. We know that we have broken his law. Because God's moral code is buried within our hearts, we cannot deny it. We can try to ignore it, numb it or shout it down, but the awareness that all is not right with us never leaves. This is not just true of some people. It's in all of us. The Bible is clear, "All have sinned and fallen short of the glory of God" (Rom. 3:23). All of us are breakers of the moral code. None of us has lived as we ought to. We have all sinned against God.

Many people reject Christianity because they think it's a religion about following a bunch of rules. They give up on God because they think they could never be good enough for him. They're partly right. On our own, we're not good enough to get to God. In fact, we're not all that good at measuring up to anyone. I might be better than Hitler, but I'm not as good as Mother Teresa, so I fall short after all. If you read what Mother Teresa wrote, she felt totally inadequate to stand before God. The Bible does not advise us to compare ourselves to each other in order to see how we are doing. We are told to consider how we are under God's law, this moral code we have been talking about. Under God's law, we are all guilty. That's where the expression, "nobody's perfect" comes from.

This is when Christianity starts to make the most sense. According to the Bible, God knew we could never be good enough for him. That's where the Gospel—the "good news" of the Christian message, comes in. We will get to that in a moment.

I conclude this section by reiterating that I believe that Christian morality is the most humble of all moral codes. I say this because Christianity does not allow any room for anyone boasting over anyone else. There is no moral high ground amongst humans. We have all blown it in some way. That is the troubling part to question three. Moving on, it gets even more troubling before it gets better.

## *4. Destiny—Where Am I Headed?*

Does life seem too short to you? It does to me. I think I'm not alone. I feel this way because I notice that once you hit a certain age, no one seems okay with getting old. We try to downplay our birthdays or keep our age a secret. People who think life is too short are always amazed at how big the little ones are getting and how old the younger ones get. Nothing is ever long enough when life is too short. Vacations, the Christmas season, and line-ups at the Passport office (okay, the last one is plenty long enough but you get the point).

One theory of why we are so afraid of getting older is because we are afraid of dying. Why are we afraid of dying? Because we have never done it before. The sudden stop at the end of one's life seems terrifying to many.

The book of Hebrews warns us about our destiny, "And just as it is appointed for man to die once, and after that comes judgment…" (Heb. 9:27). From that judgment comes one of two destinies for us, as Daniel 12:2 points out, "And many of those who sleep in the dust of the earth shall awake, some to everlasting life, and some to shame and everlasting contempt."

If you have been following along all four of life's biggest questions, question number four really just flows out of the consequences of the first three. If a person's origins are from God and they were born in order to come to know God, that is the meaning of their life. A well-lived life would be lived in relationship with God, in joyful submission to his laws. The destiny of such a life would be a relationship with God that goes on for eternity.

If we have failed to acknowledge God, find our deepest meaning in God and live in accordance with his moral plan for our lives, then our fate would understandably be to drift further and further away from him. This second scenario, I suggest, is the option that all of us have chosen. We have failed to love, worship and obey God as we ought. The consequence of this failure is to spend eternity in a place of "shame and everlasting contempt," popularly known as Hell.

One of the reasons I am a Christian is because this reasoning makes sense. God created a place like Hell for those who want nothing to do with him. God created a place like Hell for those who deserve the just punishment for the hell they made on Earth. While I may not like the idea of Hell, I completely understand the logic of there being such a place. It is not hard for me to admit that, as a consequence of the way I have lived my own life on Earth, I deserve to spend eternity in Hell, paying for my own rebellion against God.

Another reason I am a Christian is because though Hell exists, by the grace of God, I will not have to spend eternity there paying for my sin. John 3:16 is my soul's only hope and my heart's greatest treasure: "For God so loved the world, that he gave his only Son, that whoever believes in him should not perish but have eternal life."

God sent his Son to Earth to come and pay the price for our sin. By dying on a cross, Jesus paid the penalty for our sin against God in full. Jesus was fully God as well as fully human, but without sin. He was a perfect substitute to pay the price that we deserved to pay.

There is an illustration in the world of ice hockey to help you understand what Jesus did on the cross for us. In hockey, when a goalie is penalized for breaking some rule, the referee calls a penalty for the infraction. The offence has been committed and no good behaviour on the account of the goalie can wipe it way. But rather than have the team's goalie sit in the penalty box himself, an innocent teammate comes off the bench to serve the goalie's penalty. It is clear that Jesus is innocent and we are all the goalies. On the cross, Jesus was punished so that we could continue on. The Bible makes it clear that the cost of our sin is death (Rom. 6:23). Rather than making us pay for the wrongs we have done, Jesus paid that death so that we could receive his offer of eternal life. Forgiveness for our sin cost Jesus the agony of the cross.

In God's economy, sin must be paid for. Either we pay for our sin or we ask Jesus to pay for it. The Christian asks Jesus to forgive his or her sin and no longer needs to worry about being punished for it. They can now focus on living the "eternal life" that is promised in John 3:16. This eternal life starts the moment anyone commits to following Jesus. Immediately, their destiny is changed.

Other religions will tell you about the things you must do if you want to get to God. Christianity is different. It is the story of what God did to get to you. By sending Jesus to die on a cross for your sins, God offers you a gift. A gift is not earned. A gift is offered with no strings attached. It comes at the expense of the one giving, not the one receiving. We know that gifts must be opened. The choice is ours. What will we do with the gift God offers? Will we accept it or reject it? That part is our call. That part is how we figure out our destiny.

## The Life Hack You Need the Most

Many years ago, Stephen Covey wrote a bestselling book called the "7 Habits of Highly Effective People". He argued that effective people are able to prioritize their lives so that the big things of life, the things that matter most are taken care of first. Covey said too many of us get so focussed on the little, mundane things that we do not have space in our lives for what really matters. He illustrated with the now famous example of putting items in a jar. The important things of life were represented by big rocks and the less important were likened to sand and water. Covey argues that when we prioritize the unimportant demands of life we are filling our jar with sand and water. Once that is done, the jar is full and there is no room for what truly matters in life. The result is that we end up missing out on what gives life meaning.

Some might think that our relationship with God is one of those big rocks. It sort of is, but it sort of isn't. I think that a worldview, in this case, Christianity, is not one of the big rocks but rather it is the jar itself. Christianity gives us a container for storing every aspect of our existence. It gives us a framework for determining what is important and what isn't. It tells us about our origin, the meaning of life, the justification for morality and it gives us hope in our destiny.

Christianity is the jar that gives understanding to these four enormous philosophical topics. I hope these topics got you thinking, talking (and praying). I have argued that when considering what is important in your life, you need to figure out your relationship with God first of all. God is the Creator of your life. The evidence is there, and the implications make life full of meaning! To find God is to find our heart's deepest longings fulfilled. God not only meets our needs, he gives us boundaries for our choices. Finally, when we follow Jesus, trusting his death on the cross to forgive us for our sin, we have the promise of eternal life with him. That's how Christianity speaks so well into the questions of origin, meaning, morality and destiny. The Christian message not only answers life's four biggest questions, it reconciles us to God. While the Christian message may seem controversial, like that first button on your shirt, getting it right is the Life Hack you can't afford to miss.

## LIFE HACK #2
# MAKE EACH DAY COUNT

*God, there is nothing I won't give up for you. There is no distance I would not travel for you. There is nothing I would not do for you…*

This was the prayer I prayed when I became a Christian. I was about seven at the time. To be honest, I had no idea what I was talking about.

Those early years of being a Christian are mostly forgotten. Not that everything that happened was forgettable. It was just too long ago. What I mostly remember as a kid was the importance of "getting big". That seemed to be the goal of my life. My friends and I were always admiring people that were bigger and older. There was so much more they could do. Grown ups always assured me that I was on the right track. "Look how grown up you are getting," they would comment.

"So far, so good," I would think. The grown up life was well on its way.

Now that I am a "grown up," I confess that it is not at all what I imagined. Life did not work out as I thought it would. At the time of writing this book, I do not own a flying car, nor do I live in a gold house, nor do I work as a video game tester.

Life Hacks

For so many years all I wanted was to be a grown-up, but now that I am a "grown-up" I wouldn't mind going back to being a kid again. I would love to have all my meat cut up for me, have someone pay all my bills and insist I set aside some time every day for napping.

I played a lot of hockey growing up. Hockey was our family sport. My dad played, my brother played, my friends all played. We had two seasons in the Morrison house: ice hockey season in the winter and road hockey season in the summer. During those hockey-playing days, I held a misconceived belief that things would get better as soon as I got a little further. For example, in Peewee, I couldn't wait to play Bantam. In Bantam, I dreamed of playing at the Junior B level. In Junior B, I thought my problems would pass once I got to play Junior A. In Junior A, I dreamed of the day I would play college hockey.

One day I realized that it was not my league that needed to mature, it was my attitude. My problem was not the league, the coach, or the team. Regrettably, I let so much of a formative time of my life pass by never having felt peace through a single day of it. It is scary to think that some people not only go through a few years like this, but their entire lives! Have you ever caught yourself thinking this way?

*Things will be better as soon as I graduate.*

*I will be much happier once I'm in university. Or when I get my degree. Or when I get into the right career. Or when I get married. Or when we have kids. Or once I retire…*

*Perhaps things will be better when I'm dead.*

When does it end?

The end starts with today.

Isn't it haunting to think that you could live your whole life for a tomorrow that never comes? The sooner you can cease this way of thinking, the sooner you can make a fresh start with your life.

The Life Hack in this chapter is about embracing each day as it comes. Get this and you will discover the adventurous, worry-free life that God has for you. You will discover the often untapped foundation of joy known as contentment. Contentment is learning to live in every God-given moment of every God-given day. Right now is the only reality you know and can live in. Think about it! The past has already happened and will never happen again. The future is always a day away. "Tomorrow" is always one day out of your reach. All you have is right now.

And now.

And now.

And now I am clearly wasting your time.

Jonathan Edwards lived over 250 years ago. He was a brilliant philosopher and a fiery preacher who worked a circuit around the American colonies in the eighteenth century. Edwards is a hero in my books because he lived his entire life to the fullest as God's messenger. Perhaps one of the most influential preachers in America's history, Jonathan Edwards enjoyed success because he made resolutions in his early twenties to live intentionally for God and God alone.

Here are three of Edwards' famous resolutions that, if properly adapted to your own life, will guide you as you resolve to seize each day:

> *Resolution #5:* "Resolved, never to lose one moment of time; but improve my life the most profitable way I possibly can."
>
> *Resolution #6*: "Resolved, to live with all my might, while I do live."
>
> *Resolution #17*: "Resolved, that I will live so, as I shall wish I had done when I come to die." [12]

Would you like to be able to live your life like Jonathan Edwards? Imagine living like each day counted so that you could look back and know you gave it all you had.
One day we will slow down and reflect on how we have lived our lives. We will have hours to replay seasons of life in our minds and in stories we tell

---

[12] Taken from John Piper. *Don't Waste Your Life*. (Crossway Books, 2003) (This is to match your format on p.20 and 29)

to others. Imagine living your life in such a way that when you played it back you had no regrets.

We will look at two factors that keep us from achieving this. The first deals with the life behind you, and the second is the life ahead.

## When The Past Haunts Your Present

The beautiful thing about being a Christian is that you never have to allow all the garbage from the road behind you to get flung onto where you walk today. Look at what the writer of Hebrews says: "Their sins and lawless acts I will remember no more" (Hebrews 10:17). The Bible promises that, because of what Jesus has done on the cross for us, our sins are not remembered by God. Another passage tells us that God has cast our sins "as far as the east is from the west" (Psalm 103:12). You do not have to be a geography major to know that the east never meets the west. We will never be reacquainted with our sin of the past. In Christ, it is gone forever.

We must not let guilt and shame from the past rob us of the joy Jesus offers us today. If you have confessed your sin to him, your past is cleansed and your sin is forgiven.

Learn from mistakes but do not dwell on them. Can you imagine a runner who runs his race constantly looking behind him? Of course not! He looks forward to where he is going — his destination. To paraphrase Paul in Phil. 3:13-14, we need to forget what is behind us and press on towards the goal to which God has called us.

Now that I've shown why we should not be preoccupied with the past and how to make each present moment count, we can start looking ahead. Sometimes the "ahead" part can be even more problematic than the stuff behind. What do you do when the future is so unsettling?

## The Crisis of Worry-Filled Dreams

Having a goal for your life is important. I would never think to drive my car without having a destination in mind. Once I choose a place to go, I need to start planning the route. We need to have goals for our lives —

dreams you think God wants you to accomplish while on earth. Guys, this is especially important if you want to attract a girl. She will be attracted to a compelling vision for your life, but exponentially more so, *her dad* will demand you have a compelling vision for your life.

What do you worry about most?

> *What am I supposed to do with my life?*
> *What if I don't get into the school I want?*
> *What if I don't get a good job?*
> *What if I don't get married?*
> *What if I miss out on God's will for my life?*

What if, what if, what if… I've seen these two words cause countless people to lose countless days or even entire years of their lives. Human beings are worry factories: We are constantly inventing new things to worry about. We worry about our finances, our jobs, our image, our loved ones and our health, to name just a few.

Reflecting on my life, I see that it was not being a pastor, husband, father or home owner that has given me that most anxiety —it was playing hockey as a goalie. There are few places in life when you have to stand all on your own having hard rubber disks flying at you in front of a thousand paying customers. Everyone has an opinion about the goalie. They always feel free to offer their opinions freely. On top of that, all of the goalie's mistakes are being counted on an scoreboard each night. I confess to feeling anxiety about my future during that time. Would I play well enough to stay on the team?; would I get a scholarship? Is hockey the path I am supposed to be travelling along?

To fight the worry, I had Proverbs 3:5–6 painted on the front of my goalie mask. It was to serve as a daily assurance that God was in control of my life. Every time I put on my mask, I was reminded that I could rest on the promise that God was taking care of both my present and future. This popular verse, one of my favourites in the Bible, reads, "Trust in the Lord with all of your heart and lean not on your own understanding. In all of your ways acknowledge him and he will make your path straight."

The Bible tells us that if you are trusting God, you need not worry about figuring everything out. Isn't that the most liberating bit of information that those of us worriers need to hear? Here's the good news: You do not have to be anxious anymore. Jesus promises that God is ultimately concerned with taking care of you. This is what Jesus said about worry in his famous "Sermon on the Mount."

> So do not worry, saying, 'What shall we eat?' or 'What shall we drink?' or 'What shall we wear?' For the pagans run after all these things, and your heavenly Father knows that you need them. But seek first his kingdom and his righteousness, and all these things will be given to you as well. (Matt. 6:33)

As a father to two daughters, I would never imagine not providing for all their needs. I take great delight in making sure they know they are loved through making sure they have a home and food. Granted, I do not always give them everything they want — that is something else entirely. The point is that any dad worth his salt wants to and delights in providing for his children. That is just a glimpse of what God feels for us, Jesus says. Worry is a direct assault against the father-heart of God.

## When It Is Understandable to Worry

In our previous passage, Jesus mentioned that pagans, those who do not worship one God, can be consumed by worry. Let me explain what that looks like in the life of one of my friends.

In the winter of 2013 I had an opportunity to travel with a group of students in a public school program called *Students Without Borders*. Together we travelled around the country of Panama, seeing its beautiful sites and visiting with the wonderful people. One conversation I had with a grade twelve student gave me some helpful insight. Sarah was about to enter the final semester of high school and was unsure about what her life would look like afterwards. Her parents, friends and teachers all had an idea of what she should do. It seems that Sarah was the only one who did not know. This was a catalyst for anxiety. On top of that, her future seemed incredibly uncertain. To the rest of the world, Sarah had no reason to worry. She was incredibly smart, beautiful and popular. With all that going for her, she still had no clue what path she should pursue. Going to one university would lead to one career path, which may or may not lead her to find the right guy to marry. What if there were another university, or career, or a different guy to marry? Sarah faced a paralysis of analysis. There was too much to choose from and she felt the weight of the upcoming decisions.

Knowing that I was a Christian, Sarah confessed that it would be much easier for me to make decisions. After all, as someone who believes that God has a plan for our lives, it would be very comforting to know that God is leading you along that plan. Christians have the luxury of knowing that God is in control and even promises to make good of our bad decisions.

Sarah was right. If there is no God and if we alone are in control of our lives, it can be troubling. Atheists have every right to worry because they have no reason *not* to be concerned about their future. This is why they worry about making sure they go to the right school right away to get the right job with the right salary and the right retirement package. It's all about control. They have no one else to trust but themselves, and that is a lot of weight to bear. I could not bear it myself. Considering the certainty that Jesus promises, all this weight is bearable.

Because God is trustworthy, you need not let worry steal your joy for one more day. With God as your leader, even when confusion is at its peak, there can always be a certainty in your *un*certainty. To be certain of God's character and His goodness to us means that we can look uncertainty in the eye and even flourish in it. Worry can be transformed into excited anticipation of what is to come.

Here's an interesting case study from the New Testament about someone who struggled with trusting God's leading.

# Paul's Certainty in Uncertainty

The Bible gives us a backstage pass as to how the Apostle Paul, the great missionary, planned his future in regards to his destination and message. This story is from Acts 16:6–10:

> Paul and his companions traveled throughout the region of Phrygia and Galatia, having been kept by the Holy Spirit from preaching the word in the province of Asia. When they came to the border of Mysia, they tried to enter Bithynia, but the Spirit of Jesus would not allow them to. So they passed by Mysia and went

> down to Troas. During the night Paul had a vision of a man of Macedonia standing and begging him, 'Come over to Macedonia and help us.' After Paul had seen the vision, we got ready at once to leave for Macedonia, concluding that God had called us to preach the gospel to them.

To me, this passage in Acts is a comedy sketch of biblical proportions. The more I think about this text, the more I realize that Paul, the one responsible for the spread of the early church and for writing most of the New Testament, wasn't always sure what he was supposed to be doing all the time.

It is safe to suggest that there were times when Paul had no idea where God was leading him. At first he was certain that he was to minister in Asia, but then God put the brakes on that journey and it was over to Bithynia. Then he was directed otherwise by Jesus himself to go elsewhere.

Paul seemed fine with keeping his eyes on Jesus and his plans flexible. Unlike us, Paul did not let worry take over his plans for the future. What was Paul's secret? Paul lived his whole life in obedience to where he felt the Spirit of Jesus was telling him to go. Paul's heart was pointed straight at Jesus and that meant he was always in a good place regardless of where it took him. When Paul did not know where he was going, he knew who he was following. Because he knew Jesus would always take care of him, he did not freak out or take matters into his own hands.

It sounds honourable to talk like you have your entire life mapped out with each day planned. There's no problem with making plans and having goals; however, as followers of Jesus we have to keep in mind that God is free to change the course or destination as he so chooses. That's why we are followers of Jesus, not followers of our own plans.

In a 1943 letter to his friend Arthur Greeves, C.S. Lewis wrote these words:

> The great thing, if one can, is to stop regarding all the unpleasant things as interruptions of one's 'own' or 'real life'. The truth is of course that what one calls the interruptions are precisely one's real

life - the life God is sending one day by day: what one calls one's real life is a phantom of one's own imagination.[13]

This is about living the real life that God gives you each day. It's not the ideal life or the imagined life. The Life Hack is to live each moment of each day, year in and year out, knowing that God is in control. This God loves you more than you could imagine.

## Living Fully in the Moment

I am only slowly coming to grips with what it means to live fully in the moment — neither dwelling on the past nor fretting about the future. I am inspired by men like Jonathan Edwards who have radically influenced the intentionality with which I live my life. Seizing the day does not just happen; it takes a strong commitment and determined follow through.

If you can live like this chapter proposes, you will never have to look back and wonder where the great days of your youth went. When you are all grown up with a career, screaming children, car payments and a mortgage to pay, you won't wonder where your carefree, stress-free youthful days went. When you are old and grey, you will never have to sit back in your rocking chair and think your life was wasted. I have heard it said that you should live your life so well that when you are old and replay it through your memory, it will be an enjoyable experience.

In those days, you will have the satisfaction of knowing you accepted and lived each stage of life to its fullest potential. What a blessing it would be to make such a claim! It is possible.

If you are a Christian, the Bible is clear about how you deal with worry — you don't worry about it. To worry, is to not trust God. Not trusting in God is sin. The sin of pride is thinking that you know better than God. To worry about something is to say, in essence, "God, even though you promise to take care of me, I do not really think that you know and do what is best. I think that I know what is best and if what I want does not happen, I will be devastated." Pride is not acknowledging that God is sovereign over the world and "works all things according to the counsel of his will" (Eph. 1:11).

---

[13] C.S. Lewis. *Yours, Jack.* (HarperOne, New York, N.Y. April, 2008).

The truth is that none of us is wise enough to know our best future. We do not have the vision to see around every corner and into the future. But God does. He is both wise and eternal. This means he knows what is best and sees everything that is coming. God does not want these worries to cloud our vision of tomorrow. He wants us experiencing joy today. If God is who he says he is, then he has control of all the tomorrows and we need not worry about them one more day.

## LIFE HACK#3
# GET KICKED OUT OF COOL

You have a limited amount of breaths that you will take in your life. What do you want to do with the rest of the breaths you take on earth?

That's a much more intense way of asking the question we are often asked when we are young, "*"What do you want to do when you grow up?"* As kids, we had big dreams for our lives. What did you dream about doing "when you grew up"? I'm talking about after those really early years when all you wanted to be was Sponge Bob or the colour orange. What did you see yourself being? Astronaut, Doctor, Rock Star, Professional Athlete, Explorer, Dancer, Video Game Tester, Movie Star, Artist, Teacher, Plumber; all are popular options when we are kids. One day we make it through high school and graduate, still trying to hold on to our childhood dreams, wondering if they are actually attainable. Walking across the stage on grad night, we are ready to do great things with our lives; we are optimistic about making it all happen.

Some people actually follow through on their dreams. Others do not. Why do some people see their dreams become reality while others merely settle for second or third best? Something happens as we go through life that makes us want to give up on following the exciting and meaningful dreams we have. Let's be honest: it is a lot easier to go with the crowd and do what everyone else is doing than to go it alone into some new territory that only we can find. To me, that's settling for a life that is second best to what God has made you for. To too many people, that's just how they live. You can be different!

There is a medical condition called "Failure To Thrive" which is diagnosed in infants who are not able to gain weight or experience physical growth over a period of time. Failure To Thrive (FTT) is an interesting title, one that could be given to many of us adults too. Are there any adults in your life right now that you would diagnose with FTT? Please do not point. Just ask the question: *What do you think got them there?* What will stop you from catching this highly contagious pandemic sweeping through the suburban populace?

This is my made-up story theorizing how competent, rational people fail to thrive. It may assist you in avoiding the temptation to settle. You can use parts of the story to evaluate the choices and values in your life.

## The Parable of Jamie and Jenny

Jamie was a bright honour roll student who graduated from high school really excited about all the new freedom he had gained. Freed from the shackles of institutionalized education, Jamie could do anything with his life. He was excited to start pursuing things he was truly passionate about. Music was Jamie's main passion; he loved listening to it, playing it and teaching others how to play some of the many instruments he played. In grade ten, Jamie was told by his teacher that many kids in poor communities could not afford music lessons because of the high cost of teachers. Jamie's dream since that conversation was to set up a music school in a poor community so kids could get a good musical education and find hope in overcoming poverty's cycle through their music. Jamie understood this career path wasn't going to make him much money, but it was going to make the world better and that's what mattered to our budding hero.

# Get Kicked Out of Cool

The summer after grad, Jamie's dad got him a job cutting grass for the city and, for the first time in his life, he was starting to accumulate money. Every day he showed up for work in his ten year old car and his work buddies made fun of him. Because nobody likes being made fun of, he committed to saving up enough for a down payment on a new truck. After making a small down payment, Jamie took out a five-year loan to pay off the rest. His friends liked the truck and, a few high-fives later, Jamie was officially welcomed into the world of "Cool".

The problem with Jamie's entrance into the world of Cool was that it was an all-demanding world. You can't just be Cool in one place; you have to be Cool in all parts of life. Sure, Jamie's truck may have earned him some street credit with his coworkers, but they soon found something new to tease him about — his old cell phone.

Jamie's phone was *more than two years old*. His friends had the latest and greatest technology. Not wanting to fall behind, Jamie went to the mall and locked himself into a three-year contract with the phone company so he too could have a nice new phone. At the mall, Jamie picked up a new shirt and shoes because his old ones were no longer acceptable weekend attire in the world of Cool. He paid for them on his credit card knowing that he would be able to wear the clothes today with the money he would make tomorrow.

Years later, Jamie was still at his city job locked into payment plans for his truck, cell phone and credit card. He still had the dream of one day opening up a music school for poor students, but that was a few years away. Though working for the city was not his favourite line of work, it would not be long until he finally got started on his music school.

Jamie found himself a nice girlfriend named Jenny who was also from the world of Cool and, a couple years later, they got married. They committed to having their wedding in the land of Cool, even though Cool weddings cost much more than weddings anywhere else. The tough part about a Cool wedding is that everything had to be more lavish and Cool than the previous wedding. There was always a great deal of pressure on the bride to outdo the last Cool bride — to have nicer dresses, a classier venue, fancier decorations, more tender meat, etc. As a result, the cost of Cool weddings continued to go up and up, and the pressure to impress Cool friends and Cool family created a bunch of tension for Jamie and Jenny — especially when it came to paying for it all.

Not wanting to be kicked out of Cool for having a shameful wedding, Jamie and Jenny pulled off the finest Cool wedding ever seen. Thankfully, Jamie got a promotion at the city and was able to use his wage increase to help ease some of the financial burden. The only trade off was that he needed to work longer hours at the office. He still didn't like his job, but it would help pay the bills and keep his Cool new wife happy— for a while.

With the promotion came a change in friends for Jamie. No longer did he work with grass cutting teenagers. He found himself fraternizing with a group of middle class adults whose favourite topics included "The State of the Market" and "What colour to paint the new garage door." Jamie realized that he had discovered a new class in the world of Cool: *Homeowners*. Being a non-homeowner, Jamie found himself slowly being filtered out of Cool. Unless Jamie and Jenny moved quickly, other Cool people would replace them.

Jamie and Jenny quickly called up a realtor and bought a house. Like the truck, the phone, the wedding and pretty much everything else they had bought, Jamie and Jenny learned that in the world of Cool, you could easily buy stuff now and pay for it later. Jamie agreed to work at his city job a little longer to cover the mortgage. It would be paid off in twenty-five years, leaving enough time afterwards to start the music school for poor kids.

The neighbours in the Cool area were very nice. They talked about the weather and shiny new things they had bought or wanted to buy: cars, BBQs, TVs. Jamie wanted badly to talk about shiny things too, so he took out another loan and bought two nice shiny cars. Soon enough, he and Jenny were active participants in the Cool neighbourhood shiny car talk.

Jamie had to work more to pay for the cars and no longer had time to play music. Now he only played the radio on the way to and from work. Jamie and Jenny made it a tradition to watch TV shows every night as a way to relax after their long days of work. During their favourite shows, Jamie and Jenny saw all sorts of Cool ads with Cool people doing Cool things. Like the average couple in Cool, they would see over 3,000 of these ads per day. The ads promised that if Jamie and Jenny bought these new Cool things, they would be happy and Cool for their whole lives.

Jamie wanted a Cool new TV; Jenny wanted a Cool dress; Jamie wanted a Cool new laptop; Jenny wanted a Cool kitchen. To afford these things, they each decided to work just a little harder and just a little longer.

Eventually Jamie and Jenny had some Cool kids. They bought Cool clothes and pushed them around in Cool strollers. Of course all these Cool things took more money and more work to buy, but that was the price everyone was paying to be a part of Cool in those days. It was okay because they always found new credit cards to help buy Cool things.

Jamie and Jenny were soon drowning in house payments, car payments, credit card payments, and the interest that went along with each of them. Trying to keep up with it all left the couple exhausted, and each wondered how living in Cool had become so expensive and tiring. Jamie didn't even have the energy to talk about opening a school anymore.

Their kids grew up and were told they could dream big dreams and do whatever they wanted with their lives. Jamie was filled with great hope when his son, Jake, said that when he grew up he wanted to open up a music school for poor kids to get lessons.

But until then, Jake bought a Jeep and took a job that his dad got him cutting grass for the city...

That's the end of this parable. If we were doctors, we might diagnose Jamie and Jenny with having OCD — *Obsessive Comparison Disorder*.[14] The land of Cool is all about keeping up with comparisons. These comparisons create expectations that kill our contentment in life. Sadly, they are all based on a lie. Let me explain where the Land of Cool originated.

---

[14] I still vehemently argue that the real OCD should be *CDO* since that is the correct alphabetical order.

Life Hacks

## The Land of Cool Is a Lie

What if, at some point, Jamie and Jenny had realized that their entire lives were part of a big lie? Many years ago, the U.S. public broadcasting channel, PBS, aired a documentary called *Merchants Of Cool*,[15] which gave the public a backstage pass into how big corporations manipulate what is "cool" in order to get us to buy whatever it is they are selling. They know that consumers love cool. Cool is what drives the consumer economy! The problem with cool is that it started inside a market research office. A bunch of people in business suits got together and brainstormed ways to shape our culture with cool. *Merchants Of Cool* reports that the primary culture makers in Western society are five major corporations who are all vying for the hundreds of billions of dollars in consumer spending each year (the vast majority coming from teenagers). If these businesses can convince the public, through mainstream media, celebrity endorsements and other tactics, that their product is "cool," then we, the public, will respond by throwing our billions of dollars directly at them. I suppose that if we are all stupid enough to continually hand them our money, I can't really blame them for picking it up and putting it in the bank. They are good businessmen.

Media critic, Mark Crispin-Miller, summarizes how the market of Cool taps into a common human condition:

> You know, advertising has always sold anxiety and it certainly sells anxiety to the young. It's always telling them that they are not thin enough, they're not pretty enough, they don't have the right friends, or they have no friends... they're losers unless they're cool. But I don't think anybody, deep down, really feels cool enough, ever.[16]

All Jamie and Jenny had wanted was not to be losers, and to hang onto their friends by keeping up with what everyone else was doing. In reality, they were just puppets who had traded their unique hopes and dreams for

---

[15] For more information on *Merchants of Cool* check out the website (http://www.pbs.org/wgbh/pages/frontline/shows/cool/view/)

[16] See interview at: http://www.pbs.org/wgbh/pages/frontline/shows/cool/interviews/crispinmiller.html. Accessed March 17, 2009.

credit cards. It did not happen overnight either. For this fictitious couple, one decision to be cool led to another and, all of a sudden, their lives got very predictable and boring. Wake up, go to work, watch TV, and go to bed. Next day: wake up, go to work, watch TV, and go to bed. Next day: wake up...

You get the idea. At some point, if you're Jamie, you wake up wondering, What has happened to my life? Where did my dreams go? Why did I buy all this stuff? Who told me that I needed it all?

Jesus said, "I have come that you may have life and have it to the full" (John 10:10). Fullness of life, excitement and adventure— that is Jesus' offer. The problem is that we do not all choose that kind of life.

A man named E.E. Cummings once said, "To be yourself in a world that is trying to make you like everyone else is to fight the hardest battle anyone can fight."

Mark my words, without a fight your life *will* become boring, predictable and just like everyone else's. I think too many people in our culture are content just hanging out in the land of Cool. It slowly kills them, but they're okay with that because it's what they are told is normal and they just want to blend in. I like how *The Message* paraphrase of a verse from 1 Peter describes the contrast between the sacredness of our life and the tragedy of a wasted one:

> Your life is a journey you must travel with a deep consciousness of God. It cost God plenty to get you out of that dead-end, empty-headed life you grew up in. He paid with Christ's sacred blood (1 Peter 1:18).

Our culture supports the dead-end, empty-headed living this verse is talking about. Jesus wants to save you from it. He gave his life to save yours. If you do not make a conscious effort to fight it, you will write the exact same story as Jamie, Jenny and so many others that you and I know well.

## Be Unique, Just Like Everybody Else

I once heard Donald Miller, *NY Times* bestselling author, speak about what characterizes a good story. Miller argued that, in order for a story to be worthwhile, the protagonist must have a compelling objective. A story about a guy buying a car is not as exciting for an audience as a story about a guy who *drives* a car, risking his life to stop a bomb from going off in a crowded mall. Think about the objective of your life. What are you trying to accomplish? If your life were a movie, would anybody want to go see it? If not, you probably are telling a lame story with your life.

"Oh wow... so he finally managed to pay off his mortgage, retire, and play golf (wipe away a tear)... that's... that's just a beautiful story."

That never happens.

We have all watched a great preview for a movie and anticipated its release. This is the kind of preview where you whisper to your friend, "We have to see that movie!" When you finally get to watch it in the theatre, you find out it is actually a real stinker. What a disappointment!

Nobody ever leaves a movie theatre at the end of a bad movie and concludes, "Well, that's it! All movies are meaningless!" Instead we walk out and conclude, "*That* movie was meaningless."

If your life seems like it lacks excitement, adventure or anything worth remembering, do not conclude that *all life* is meaningless! It just might be that, so far, *your* life has been meaningless.

A better response would be to conclude that your movie has, so far, had a slow beginning. That happens with many great movies. As long as you still have breath and the credits have not started rolling, you still have time to salvage your story. In order to do this, you need to find where the story lost the plot.

How did you get to this point? Your preview was good. It had potential. You were young, had some profound ideas, and you had the courage to do something about them. However deep it has been buried, that potential is still there. In the next chapter we will dig it up together. For now, let's continue to look at why people keep the adventure buried.

We lose our original God-given dream and settle for a meaningless life when we try to live in Cool. In Jesus' parable of the sower, we are like the young seed that fell among thorns. It springs up into a plant but is soon choked by the cares of the world (Matt. 13:22). When plants choke, they wither and die. This plant bears no fruit as it was intended to. It has become useless. Given the seed's enormous potential, this is a tragedy.

Jesus taught us that the road to Hell is wide and easy to find — just do what everyone else is doing. There is also a narrow road. It is smaller and tougher to find, but it leads to the life you really want to live. The way to finding this narrow road is to know that God did not make you to be like everyone else. He made you incredibly unique for unique purposes. Long before you were born, God had a plan for you — the one and only you in the history of the world (Ps. 139:13). The Bible is clear that God crafted you with distinct gifts and abilities. Then he lined up a fingerprint, some DNA, and laid out experiences that would ensure you were one of a kind. Ephesians 2:10 compares us to a work of art. We are God's workmanship, his masterpiece.

How seriously does God take it that we use our God-given uniqueness to its fullest potential? Let's look at what he said to a bunch of people who were not living up to their full potential.

## A Lesson From the Laodiceans

The more I learn about the book of Revelation, the more I think it is one of the greatest yet all too often misunderstood gems of the New Testament. Revelation 3:17–22 is a letter written to the Church in a city called Laodicea. In it we see Jesus' sharp rebuke of a church that was so rich and in love with its culture that it had become useless to him and his purposes for them. Jesus invites his people, "Here I am, I stand at the door and knock" (Rev. 3:20). That's interesting. Jesus was not present at a meeting that was called in *his name*. Picture the King of all kings and Lord of all lords standing outside knocking on the door of this humble mud structure waiting for someone to let him in.

While I studied at Oxford, I often visited a piece of art that hangs on one of the chapel walls at Keble College. It is called, "The Light Of The World" and was painted by Holman Hunt in the middle of the nineteenth century. In this famous painting, Jesus stands outside a door overgrown with vines and (obviously) unopened for a long time. With a more careful look, the observer notices that Jesus knocks on the door *because there is no handle on the outside.* The door can only be opened from within. Whoever is inside seems to be uninterested in the one patiently waiting to enter.

This scene reminds me of the closing credits of the old cartoon from my childhood called, *The Flintstones*. Set in the prehistoric age, at the end of each episode, Fred puts the family cat outside for the night, only to have the cat jump back into the house to close and lock the door. Fred is left outside for the night instead of the cat. The show ends with Fred pounding on the door of his own house yelling, "Wilma!"

We treat Jesus this way when we get so obsessed with blending in with our culture that we forget about Jesus and his counter-cultural purposes for our lives and our churches. We think we are doing just fine, but Jesus sees it a different way: "You say, 'I am rich; I have acquired wealth and do not need a thing.' But you do not realize that you are wretched, pitiful, poor, blind and naked" (Rev. 3:17).

These Christians that Jesus was talking to were very confused. Because of their great wealth, they believed they needed nothing. Jesus couldn't disagree more, choosing adjectives such as "wretched, poor, blind and naked" to describe them. This is what happens when Christians try to live in Cool - they get called out by Jesus.

> I know your works: you are neither cold nor hot. Would that you were either cold or hot! So, because you are lukewarm, and neither hot nor cold, I will spit you out of my mouth. (Rev. 3:15-16).

When I first heard these words of Jesus to the Laodiceans, they confused me. Was Jesus angry with them because they were not passionately hot or devilishly cold to the things of God? Is this verse telling us to decide whether we are *all* for Jesus or *all* against him? I was always told that Jesus wishes we would choose one but not both, and whatever we do, not to be lukewarm. Though I think that is still true (we do have to make that decision) that is not what Jesus is saying *here*.

I could never understand why Jesus would *want* people to be so devilishly cold. Was it not a sin to be cold towards God? It did not make sense to me why Jesus would want people he made and died for playing for the wrong team.

Looking more carefully at the ancient city of Laodicea, the real meaning of this passage becomes clear and convicting. Laodicea was a very affluent city, much like modern cities of the West today. Despite the wealth, the original founders built the city at a vast distance from any major body of water. This caused a big problem for people who lived there. Water is a necessity for human survival. Because they had money, the Laodiceans built expensive aqueducts to transport their water. Outside Laodicea were the hot springs of Hieropolis, whose warm water was famous for its healing powers. Think of the relaxation that comes from soaking in a hot tub. That is a picture of Hieropolis. In addition, the aqueducts from the springs of Colossae supplied Laodicea with cold spring water, ideal for a refreshing drink. The problem with transporting your water via the aqueduct system in those days was the exposure of the water to the elements during its journey. By the time the hot water arrived in Laodicea it had had time to cool and was no longer hot. The cold water from Colossae had the opposite problem— it warmed up in the sun. The hot water cooled and the cold water warmed up. Both aqueducts brought in a fresh supply of lukewarm water.

The hot water was no longer good for healing and the cold water was too warm to be refreshing. They were both useless. Nobody likes a tall glass of warm water on a hot day. You would spit that stuff out! Jesus does too.

It seems like Jesus is saying to the Laodicean church, and to all of us who are like them, "You have compromised with your culture. You have become useless for the work of God. You were supposed to be different — unique — in order to show the world what I am like. Instead, you do not look like me; you look like everyone else. So I'm going to spit you out."

Those are tough words. Jesus is serious in his desire that we live lives of purpose and effectiveness so that we can do what he created us to do.

Are you hot, cold, or lukewarm? What do you think Jesus would say if he wrote a letter to your church? What do you think Jesus would say if he wrote a letter to you?

# How to Rip Up Your Invitation to Cool

There are other Bible heroes that God called to be different; in fact, he did it constantly. Jacob, Rahab, Jonah, Isaiah, Ezekiel, Jeremiah, Esther, Hosea, Daniel, John the Baptist, and Paul are just a few of the many great men and women God asked to do some radical, often unpopular, things. Considering the trajectory of their lives and the impact they have made on world history, I would say that it was worth the price (easy to say when you're not the one paying it!). World history was forever changed because of these men and women. The problem is that they all got kicked out of Cool for how they chose to live.

My prayer is that God would raise up a generation of rebels who will reject the invitation to live in the land of Cool. They will still love Cool people, but will refuse to get sucked into their destructive habits.

God is calling rebels in our midst today. It used to be that rebels were the type who wore leather jackets, rode motorcycles, smoked cigarettes and drank cheap domestic beer. Today's rebels are people who look at their world critically and observe the ensnaring patterns of the consumeristic lifestyle. They see the empty promises of Cool for the lies they are. Today's rebels choose to live counter-culturally. They see the masses simply going along with the current, and choose instead to swim upstream no matter how tiring it may get.

## Dare to Be Different

If you're up for the challenge of being a 21st century rebel who can be a part of changing how people live their lives, I offer here a few suggestions. You may have some ideas and application points that differ from mine, but consider these six possibilities:

### 1. Live on Less

Once you figure out just how enslaving consumer culture really is, you will discover just how little you actually need. You know that new phone you think you need which does the same stuff as your old phone but has a slightly better camera and is one model newer? Before you buy something, ask yourself the tough questions: Do I really need this? What is this purchase promising to give me? Will it deliver what I am really looking for?

Picture everything you buy coming with a string that ties itself to you. The more stuff you have, the more strings get attached to you. With more strings come more restrictions and less mobility. We like to think that we own all our stuff, but actually our stuff starts to own us. We forget that everything belongs to God who gives stuff to us in order that we might take care of and share it with others who need our care. That is why those who have the least possessions are often the most generous people. They have not let their stuff own them and can freely give. A.W. Tozer calls this, "The blessedness of possessing nothing."[17] According to Tozer, there is a great blessing in owning few things. Learn to live on as little as possible and very little will own you.

I mention this because the time is coming, or maybe it has already come, when a credit card company will offer you some money that you have not earned. This offer will be your introduction to the "buy now, pay later" mentality. Be warned; this kind of offer brings with it many, many strings that a young person may not have the maturity or discipline to handle. I'm not against credit cards, but be sure you have the money to back up your spending. The Bible has a proverb which states that someone who borrows money becomes a slave to the person who loaned it to them (Prov. 22:7). We voluntarily offer ourselves in service to the credit companies from which we borrow.

Here is an equation worth remembering: Five dollars earned minus seven dollars spent = Unhappy Life.

At the least, make sure you pay off your credit card bill every month. Avoiding long-term debt will help you in the long run. Here's my advice for whatever it is worth: if you cannot pay your expenses, cut up your credit card, find some help in building a budget and pray that God would help you live within your means.

---

[17] Tozer, A.W. *The Pursuit Of God* (Christian Publications, 1993).

## *2. Be Willing to Fail*

The fear of failure keeps people living boring lives. Too many in our culture are absolutely paralyzed by a fear of failure, so they never try to live out their God-given dreams. They are scared to fail, look bad, or end up broke and living on the streets. Instead of risking failure, they settle in the Land of Cool and know nothing but the boredom of a life full of the routine, the safe and the familiar.

I grew up reading this quote from Theodore Roosevelt that my dad had posted on his wall.

> It is not the critic who counts; nor the man who points out how the strong man stumbles, or where the doer of deeds could have done them better. The credit belongs to the man who is actually in the arena, whose face is marred by dust and sweat; who strives valiantly; who errs and comes short again and again; because there is not effort without error and shortcomings… who at the best knows in the end the triumph of high achievement and who at the worst, if he fails, at least he fails while daring greatly. So that his place shall never be with those cold and timid souls who know neither victory nor defeat.[18]

I would encourage you to post it somewhere to remind you that it's okay to risk big, to fail big and to be mocked for it. At least you are among the few who try and, according to Roosevelt, for that you are worthy of honour.

Here are some encouraging stories highlighting the kind of risks that cultural-shaping leaders take. Robert Guizeta, CEO of Coca Cola from 1980–1997, has a remarkable story of overcoming failure and building one of the most recognizable brands in the world. He said, "Remember if you take risks, you may still fail, but if you do not take risks you will surely fail. The greatest risk of all is to do nothing."[19] Some people are so worried about looking bad that they will not try anything that involves any

---

[18] Theodore Roosevelt. From a speech in Paris on April 23, 1910 called "Citizenship in a Republic".

[19] See article "Risk" at www.livinglifefully.com/risk.html. Accessed June 3, 2011.

element of risk. Sure, with risk comes the potential for failure. With failure comes the potential to look bad. Failure can be a really good thing, however. I have learned some of the greatest lessons in life when I have taken the great risks, tried the impossible, and fallen flat on my face. After years of struggling to invent the lightbulb, Thomas Edison commented, "I have not failed. I've just found ten thousand ways that won't work." He eventually found a way to make it work and anyone who has had to cram for a test or write a paper long into the night is thankful for his persistence.

Here's a more encouraging story. Jonas Salk got it wrong over two hundred times trying to make a cure for polio. His 201st became the vaccine for the fatal disease. Somebody asked, "How did it feel to fail 200 times trying to invent a vaccine for polio?" His response was, "I never failed 200 times at anything in my life... I simply discovered 200 ways how not to make a vaccine for polio."

It is inevitable that you will fail at many things throughout your life. It is coming — so learn to handle failure well. Realize that when you run hard, you will sometimes fall. Only good can come from getting up each time, brushing off the dirt, cleaning up the blood and starting to run again. Be thankful that you just learned another lesson in how to run properly.

## 3. Have the Courage to Be Different

It is only my opinion but I believe that courage is one of the primary characteristics a Christian must possess in the 21st century. I know that being loving and gracious are super important, but courage today is right up there near the top with love and grace. Courage is the ability to do the right thing no matter how difficult the process may be. It takes courage to be like Daniel, who maintained his integrity as King Nebachanezzar and Ancient Babylonian culture relentlessly tried to make him compromise who he was. There is tremendous pressure to conform today. Courage is what is needed to remain true to what God is calling you to and who he is calling you to be.

It takes courage to think simply and believe in your heart that you are going to live differently. It takes courage to insist that you will not be defined by your possessions or by anything other than what God tells you that you are. If you are a Christian, the Bible says that you are a child of

God. Your true identity is not in the car you drive, the house you live in, your marital status, the amount of money in your bank account, or the clothes you wear. Those things do not make a person more or less important. They do not add to or subtract from the value found in human life. Others around you may not believe that, but it doesn't mean you have to buy in. Take courage to live in the truth of what the Bible says and learn to see others in the same light.

## 4. It's About Priorities

In January of 2009, I took a three-week trip to the country of Gambia in Africa. Going into the trip, I knew that my time there was limited. It would have been foolish of me to act as if this country were my long-term home. I didn't build a house there. I didn't buy a car, or sign a long-term cell phone contract. I was constantly aware of the brevity of my stay and that affected the way I lived each day. My conversations were more intentional; I tried to help whomever in whatever way I could. Each day was a new chance to grow in my love for God and to share his love with all who crossed my path. I could put up with not having my own bed with my own sheets and pillow; I didn't need my Starbucks coffee, and I could put up with food that I didn't like. I did this because I knew my time there was temporary and I would be home soon enough.

It's the same with Christians awaiting their home in heaven. We are to live as if this world is passing away and that heaven is our final destination. I have found that it is the people that live like this who are the most fun and exciting people to be around. They live the most rewarding lives because they don't care about rewards here on Earth. When people live for heaven, nothing can own them and nothing can stop them from their mission of knowing God and making him known. They know that to be human on Earth is not about their collection of stuff, their entertainment, or their anything. It is about Jesus and his work in others. May we all live our lives with eternity at the forefront of our minds. How different would our churches be if the people of God actually lived like this?

## 5. Practice Gratitude

At what point will you ever have enough? "Enough" is a great word that we should all adopt as our mantra when it comes to our possessions. Make a bold declaration that what you have is good enough to live on, and that adding anything else is not going to make you happy. Turn on the tap and thank God that you are among the most fortunate people in the world who can get clean drinking water from that tap. Drive your old car and be thankful that you are wealthy enough to afford it. Be grateful you have a roof over your head. Be grateful for the clothes in your closet. Be grateful for the food in your stomach and the food in the fridge. If you have meat in your sandwich tomorrow, say a prayer of thanks for the high standard of living you enjoy. You have enough. Are you grateful for it? That is the secret to living the contented life Jesus has for us.

I once saw a commercial where a guy woke up and saw his wife and kids dressed up in wrapping paper. He took away the wrapping and yelled, "A gift." As he walked around his house, everything he used was wrapped as well. He kept unwrapping these otherwise ordinary items and exclaiming, "A gift!" He unwrapped his car ("a gift"), he went to his job ("a gift") and the day continued. While I have no idea what this ad was selling, it was clearly preaching the joy of gratitude. I want to live like that.

### *6. Give More Away*

Every time you give away money or make financial sacrifices, you chip away at that big ugly monster of consumerism that has its grip on so many North Americans today. Jesus says, "Where your treasure is, there your heart will be also." Your money will follow your heart. Give to your church and watch your passion grow for the church. Give to an organization that fights poverty or disease and watch your heart begin to break for the things that break God's heart. You can be free from the tyranny of selfish consumeristic hoarding by giving away your time, talent and treasure. When you give, your attention is diverted away from yourself towards a person, a cause, or a vision much bigger than yourself. That's how you do it. Give generously and watch your heart begin to change.

## Which Road Will You Choose?

Consider the words of Russian poet, Boris Pasernak:

> It is not revolutions and upheavals
> That clear the road to new and better days,

> But revelations, lavishness and torments
> Of someone's soul, inspired and ablaze.

Pasernak has described the kind of people who make a difference in the world. They are different. So how are you going to live differently? We started this chapter by asking: *What do you want to do with the rest of the breaths you take on earth?*

There are two roads you can take these breaths on — one is wide and easy to find. It is a road with lots of traffic and soft ground underfoot. There you will find Jamie, Jenny and all their Cool friends who are consumed by conformity, consumption, safety, and worry about their image.

The second road is narrow; there are not many people walking on it because it is tough to find and hard on the feet. Those on this road value contentment, uniqueness, simplicity, clarity and sacrifice.

This is the road that leads out of the make-believe land of Cool and into true life. How will you live the rest of your one chance at life? The choice is yours.

# LIFE HACK #4
# CONSIDER YOUR CALLING

One day I made up a story about a bus driver named "Gus." I'd like to share it with you.

This is Gus. Every day for the last twenty years, Gus has driven the same route. He starts on Western Street and ends on Eastern Avenue.

Back and forth. Back and forth.

One day Gus decided that he did not want to drive that route anymore. This day he was going to take a new approach.

He would pick up passengers and ask where they needed to go.
He came to the first stop and picked up the first passengers of the day.

"Where will it be?" Gus asked.

One needed a ride to work. Another needed to get groceries. One guy asked for a lift to the ski hill.

Life Hacks

A ride to work was understandable. A trip to the grocery store was manageable. But going all the way to a ski hill? That was really out of the way. But Gus realized that as he did not have any particular route, anything could be on the way. He thought about it and agreed to make the drive.

The conditions were very tough for Gus and his bus. He made the drop off and headed back down the mountain. Along the way he stopped at a bus stop where a man with a whole bunch of penguins was waiting for a bus.

"Can you help me take all these penguins to the zoo?" asked the man.

Penguins? Gus had never done that before. Then again, he had never done any of these adventures before. Gus agreed and dropped them all off at the zoo.

Gus stopped at another stop where he met some students.

One needed a ride home. One needed a ride to a friend's house. One needed to go to the mall. Gus drove them all wherever they wanted to go. After dropping off the last student, to his amazement, the man with the penguins was standing at a bus stop.

Gus pulled over.

"I took you to the zoo like you asked!" protested Gus.

Consider Your Calling

"Yes, you did. The zoo was fun. Now I thought we would catch a baseball game."

Gus obliged and took the man with the penguins to the baseball stadium.

The day was almost over when Gus realized he should get back to his regular route.

Just before arriving at the end of the line, Gus saw his boss standing at the side of the road.

"How am I going to explain this? I'm going to be fired." Gus thought to himself.

"Gus. Is this your bus?" asked his boss.

"Yes sir."

"And Gus, is this your route?"

"Yes sir."

The boss paused. "Great. Do you mind taking a little detour. I need a lift home."

Gus paused and replied, "I don't usually do this but... Okay, hop on!"

59

# Where Would You Like To Go?

People usually take the story of Gus and his wandering bus one of two ways: some will say that Gus had an amazing adventure helping all the people he encountered. Gus himself would have confessed that he did not really know where he was going at the beginning of the day. However, because of his willingness to see his life as an unfolding adventure, he got a day full of new friends, helpful deeds, and even got to drive around a bunch of penguins. Sometimes the people who have lived the most exciting lives never knew what they were going to do "when they grew up."

Others would tell you that Gus' story is an unfortunate one. They would argue that it would have been much better if Gus had known at the outset of the day where he was going and then stuck to the plan. According to this perspective, too many people, like Gus, spend their whole lives living life only to make everyone else happy. As a result, they end up doing only what everyone else wants them to do and never actually living the way they feel they were meant to live. Their parents, teachers, friends, and society all have ideas for their life and this can become an overwhelming burden.

Would it have been better for Gus to have a vision for his life or was it better to just drive around all day? This chapter will examine this question through the filter of our "calling."

A calling is another way of about talking about what you are supposed to do with your life. It's what gets you out of bed in the morning. By the end of this chapter, you will have a better idea about what God might be asking from you for your life. We will look at two men who discovered their callings in very different ways.[20] Before we do that, there is one bit of background work we must address.

---

[20] For highlighting the contributions and stories of these two astounding men, I am in debt to my Oxford professor, Dr. Os Guinness, particularly in his article titled, "Become Who You Are." For more see Guinness, Os. *The Call* (Nashville, Tenn.: W Publishing Group, 1998).

## The Luxury of Having a Caller

Before we look at your calling, we need to consider the idea of having a *Caller*. You can only have a calling if you first have a Caller. This is the luxury of the Christian worldview. Christianity professes that behind it all there is a God who has a plan. God is carrying out that plan and he uses people to do it. This God is a being who loves you and wants to include you in what he is doing. He is the Caller.

Your primary calling is to be in relationship with God. This calling (as we learned in Chapter One) sets the tone for everything else you will ever do in life. If you want to know your primary calling, you have to first know your Primary Caller. If you miss your primary calling you will miss out on the whole reason for your existence. The Bible is very clear about God's will for your life: "For this is the will of God, your sanctification" (1 Thess. 4:3).

I hope that's not a letdown for you. Sanctification means to be "set apart" for the purposes of living a holy life before God and others. What does "being set apart" look like? We set apart things in other areas of life all the time. We set apart the recyclables and we set apart our fine dishes from the regular ones. Being set apart yourself means acknowledging that you are called to live a holy life— a life that honours God— in a world that does not.

Romans 8:29 makes God's purpose in our lives very clear. "For those whom he foreknew he also predestined to be conformed to the image of his Son…" God's will for you is to make you more like Jesus. Christlikeness is your target, your goal, your vision, and the reason you were created. You are set apart to be like Jesus. That goal will take the rest of your life to accomplish.

By this point, I bet some people feel tricked. I told you that I could tell you God's will for your life. Then I told you it was about a big word like sanctification. That never included what job you will have, who you will marry or where you will live. Are you disappointed? I know I was when I first heard how vague God's will can be. Then I realized that God primarily cares much more about the state of my soul than about my job, marital status or living arrangements. He cares more about who I am than what I do. We must be careful that we don't get too caught up in figuring out what we should be doing instead of figuring out who we should be becoming. Making little of God's priority to make us holy reveals how we are not fully convinced that following Jesus is to be the most important pursuit. Perhaps we are still more in love with the idea of being in control, being comfortable, successful, rich or famous, than we are about being like Jesus.

God gives our lives purpose, a reason to get up every morning. This, to me, is a great luxury. It is a reason to live. This is the "life to the full" that Jesus promises in John 10:10. Once you get your primary calling sorted out, you can move to the specifics of the secondary calling. As we will now see, there are a several different perspectives on how God rolls out these secondary callings. Here are two examples.

## Case Study in Calling #1: William Wilberforce

I once had the chance to visit James Island, an island on the west coast of Africa. The island is now uninhabited, but it was once a strategic slave trading post for several European countries. Taking a tour of this island was difficult to stomach as our local tour guide told several stories of the brutality that occurred because of the transatlantic slave trade that destroyed the lives of millions of African men, women and children. Today, on the mainland, stands a thirty-foot statue of a man standing with arms held high and broken chains on his wrists. An inscription below reads in bold, capital letters, "Never Again!" This triumphant sign is a picture of freedom. It declares that there will be no more Africans taken from their homes and shipped like cattle to work as slaves in other countries. Their freedom was earned by those who campaigned with all they had to end this brutal slave trade. One of those is one of my heroes: William Wilberforce.

According to his biographers, William Wilberforce was an intelligent, witty, handsome and winsome young man. He was the kind of guy who could have been successful at anything he tried. A devout Christian, Wilberforce was convinced that the most holy thing for him to do was to work in the church. Coming from a rich English family, Wilberforce was fortunate to receive an education at the University of Cambridge. There he gained wisdom and knowledge, and earned influence through his many social connections. This opened up the possibility of not just ministry, but also English politics, an area of society he seemed to naturally gravitate

Consider Your Calling

towards. What was Wilberforce to do? How do you decide what kind of path you should pursue? William Wilberforce had a tough decision to make: the church or politics?

In December of 1785, weighing his options and struggling in prayer, a confused William Wilberforce made a famous visit to see the respected English clergyman, Rev. John Newton. Newton is famously known as the slave trader who had a dramatic conversion to Christianity and then became a pastor. His transformation was so dramatic, he penned the famous words: "Amazing grace, how sweet the sound that saved a wretch like me." Newton knew that Wilberforce had been given an abundance of gifts and influence that would suit the purposes of God best in the world of politics. So this author of the most well known song in history (Amazing Grace) convinced the young William that, to make the greatest impact for God, he would be wisest to put his gifts and talents to use in the political arena where he could pursue the abolition of the slave trade.

God often uses trustworthy, wise people in our lives to steer us towards our calling. Often, other people can more clearly see our natural gifts and talents when we are deciding what path to pursue in life. These will probably be the same people who will discourage you from entering a TV singing competition. We have all witnessed too many train wreck contestants who would have saved themselves a lot of public embarrassment if they had just asked some honest friends, "Do you think I should sing on national TV?" Thankfully, Wilberforce had a friend who could speak to him honestly.

On Sunday, October 28, 1787, William Wilberforce became clear about his calling. That day he wrote these words in his journal: "God Almighty has set before me two great objects, the suppression of the Slave Trade and the Reformation Manners."[21]

These objectives would be no easy feat to accomplish. In those days, English traders made lucrative careers sailing up and down the African coast, collecting slaves to work in Europe and the Americas. Europeans captured between 35,000 and 50,000 Africans a year and shipped them across the sea and into a lifetime of cruel slavery. This was a very

---

[21] Piper, John. *Amazing Grace in the Life of William Wilberforce*. (Wheaton, Illinois: Crossway Books, 2003). P. 35.

profitable business that made many people rich and powerful.[22] Nobody was looking to give up this important cog in the eighteenth century economy. As one reporter at the time wrote, "The impossibility of doing without slaves in the West Indies will always prevent this traffic being dropped. The necessity, the absolute necessity, then, of carrying it on, must, since there is no other, be its excuse."[23]

Wilberforce was not about to let intimidation stop him. He felt called to this purpose by God and no opposition would prevent him and his friends from achieving their goal. In just four years, Wilberforce and his abolitionist sidekick, Thomas Clarkson, introduced twelve bills in the British parliament, each of them rallying against the slave trade. Each time the bills were voted down. The road towards abolition would be "blocked by vested interests, parliamentary filibustering, entrenched bigotry, international politics, slave unrest, personal sickness, and political fear."[24] Other bills introduced by Wilberforce were defeated in 1791, 1792, 1793, 1797, 1798, 1799, 1804, and 1805.

Wilberforce and the group of Christian abolitionists known as the *Clapham Sect* came up with many creative ways to campaign. Year after year they campaigned across England. One petition they drew up had more than 800,000 signatures on it. This figure was approximately ten percent of the English population at the time. The abolitionists presented the petition to Parliament by rolling the long scroll of names down the floor.[25] This visual demonstration should have had quite the effect. However, it did not have the effect they wanted. They lost the vote again that year.

---

[22] Stark, Rodney. *For the Glory Of God: How Monotheism Led To The Reformations, Science, Witch-Hunts and the End Of Slavery.* (Princeton, N.J.: Princeton University Press, 2003).

[23] Taken from Gali, Mark. *131 Christians Everyone Should Know.* (Nashville, Tenn : Christianity Today, 2000). p. 283.

[24] *Ibid*, p. 283.

[25] See tribute to William Wilberforce. Find this article at: www.wilberforcecentral.org/wfc/Wilberforce/index.html. Accessed Feb. 20, 2013.

As well as fighting slavery, Wilberforce also fought for "the reformation of morals." He wanted to see England, a supposedly Christian nation, live Christian-ly. Wilberforce set the example by giving away one-quarter of his income to fight poverty. He also campaigned to stop children being forced to work long hours in unsafe, dirty chimneys. He helped single mothers, promoted religious education in local Sunday schools, and even set up orphanages to care for abandoned children. Wilberforce and his friends founded groups like the *Society for Bettering the Cause of the Poor*, and the *Society for the Prevention of Cruelty to Animals* (SPCA).

I do not know how Wilberforce had the time to do all this. We know that such campaigning certainly took its toll on his health. He encountered waves of debilitating illness, suffering pain that could only be eased with the popular drug at the time, opium. The side effects of such a damaging drug were unknown to doctors at the time. Wilberforce became addicted, suffering from terrible hallucinations and crippling bouts of depression. Not only that, but Wilberforce was vilified by many, falsely accused of many evils, and many times his friends thought his life was in jeopardy.[26]

After a lifetime of Wilberforce's campaigning and with the help of some savvy political maneuvering by him and his allies, the British government passed *The Slave Trade Act* on March 25, 1807, a huge victory in their campaign.[27] However, it was not until July 26, 1833 that sanctions were made to officially abolish slavery across the British Empire.[28] Three days later, William Wilberforce's health quickly deteriorated and he died. His life's mission was complete and the tired leader went home to be with Jesus.

To me, William Wilberforce is a heroic example of how a human being can find his calling by combining gifts and passions, and solving a major world problem. Wilberforce felt that God had given him his education, intelligence, and influence in politics in order to fight slavery. He knew what he was called to do and never gave up doing it. History will never be

---

[26] The opposition became so fierce, one friend feared that one day he would read about Wilberforce's being "carbonated [broiled] by Indian planters, barbecued by African merchants, and eaten by Guinea captains."

[27] Pollock, John. *Wilberforce*. (New York, NY. : St. Martin's Press, 1977) P. 214.

[28] *Ibid*, p. 308.

the same because of the drive of this eighteenth century abolitionist movement. In addition, my friends in Gambia will never be the same because of what these heroes did.

Now let's look at someone who took a completely different approach to discovering the call of God on his life and what impact that call would have on the world.

## Case Study in Calling #2: Alexander Solzhenitsyn

Alexander Solzhenitsyn (1918-2008) was a Russian writer and novelist who won a Nobel laureate, the ultimate prize you can be awarded in writing. Many people have never heard of him, but he is an important historical figure. Solzhenitsyn is best known for his works, *One Day in the Life of Ivan Denisovich* and *The Gulag Archipelago* (the latter has sold over 30 million copies and has been translated into 35 languages). Solzhenitsyn is known as the man who blew the whistle on Communist Russia, informing the world of how the oppressive KGB was treating its prisoners in the Gulag (a Russian prison). Today Solzhenitsyn is a hero whose story of stumbling into his calling needs to be told.

Alexander Solzhenitsyn spent the years of 1945-1953 in Joseph Stalin's prison camps after he publicly criticized the Russian dictator's war practices. Prison was the common punishment for anyone who spoke against the Communist State. After surviving years in these horrendous, dehumanizing camps, Solzhenitsyn turned his pen into a weapon and took on the Soviet Communist regime while also giving dignity and recognition to the countless nameless and faceless people who were victimized by Russian tyranny.

How did this Nobel laureate get his start in writing? He confesses, "I drifted into literature unthinkingly, without really knowing what I needed from it, or what I could do for it. I just felt depressed because it was so difficult."[29]

Reflecting on his life and experience in the Gulag, Solzhenitsyn could see that all this stumbling was how God was preparing him for what he would

---

[29] Solzhenitsyn, Alexander. *The Oak and The Calf*. (Harper & Row Publishers, 1979).

be called on to do in his later years. When the time came for God to put the struggling Russian writer on the world's stage, he was ready. It was almost like his whole life had been in preparation for this time.

While in prison, Solzhenitsyn found himself with an abundance of material about which to write. However, under the Communist regime, censorship of all writing was strictly enforced. If only one line had been discovered, he would have been killed. All that this writer/prisoner had to report would have been instantly lost.

A medical test in 1953 revealed that Solzhenitsyn had a malignant tumour in his body. He was given three weeks to live. Frantically, he wrote everything he had in tiny letters on a scroll, rolled it up and placed it in a champagne bottle. He buried it in the prison and left for his medical treatment. His next problem was who to tell about his hidden writings. Fellow prisoners could not be trusted because of the reward for leaking information to the guards. His parents were dead, close friends were all imprisoned in other camps, and even his wife had remarried.

Feeling hopeless about the situation, Solzhenitsyn was sent away to die. Three weeks passed and, contrary to what his doctors originally had predicted, he lived. Solzhenitsyn called this a divine miracle. From that moment on, he wrote, "…all the life that has been given back to me has not been mine in the full sense: it is built around a purpose…"

Solzhenitsyn devoted the rest of his life to vindicating the experiences of those who had suffered in those camps. He felt it was his calling to bring justice to their oppressors as well. "It was not only my life's work but the dying wish of the millions whose last whisper, last moan, had been cut short on some hut floor in some prison camp."[30]

Consider the totally different approaches to calling in the stories of these two remarkable men. William Wilberforce received his calling at twenty-eight. Solzhenitsyn found his conviction much later in life. The Russian hero concludes,

---

[30] Any writer would appreciate his drive to forsake other joys and be dedicated to complete his task. He confesses, "I could have enjoyed myself so much, breathing fresh air, resting, stretching my cramped limbs, but my duty to the dead permitted no such self-indulgence. They are dead. You are alive: do your duty. The world must know about it."

> It makes me happier, more secure, to think that I do not have to plan and manage everything for myself, that I am only a sword made sharp to smite the unclean forces, an enchanted sword to cleave and disperse them.[31]

Alexander Solzhenitsyn could look back on his life and trace the path that God had been leading him on all along.

We have looked at the unfolding stories of William Wilberforce and Alexander Solzhenitsyn; two extraordinary men with two totally different experiences of how God calls a person. Which story do you think will explain the way God has called or is calling you?

## Your Secondary Calling: Where Passions, Talents and the World's Needs All Come Together

We can do some work together to help you work towards putting yourself in the best position to live out the kind of life that we are talking about — a life with meaning, purpose, and a sense of calling.

My research has revealed to me that finding meaning in something like your job is very important to Millennials (like myself)[32] We will spend roughly thirty percent of our lives at work. That is a significant portion of our life. Let's move towards finding out where the things you do well with passion can be done for a living.

The following Venn diagram could radically alter the path you are walking on. Take a piece of paper and draw three circles that all connect in the middle. In one circle write, "Things I Am Good At". In another circle write, "What I'm Passionate About." In the third, pencil in "What the World Needs." While it seems pretty straightforward, I'll give you some instructions on what to write in the rest of the circles.

---

[31] Aleksandr Solzhenitsyn, *The Oak and the Calf.* (Collins Harvill, July 1980).

[32] Sociologists tell us that a Millennial is someone born between 1980 and 2000.

Consider Your Calling

*Venn diagram labeled: DEAD END JOB, THINGS YOU ARE GOOD AT, HOBBIES, WHAT THE WORLD NEEDS, WHAT YOU'RE PASSIONATE ABOUT, YOUR SWEET SPOT*

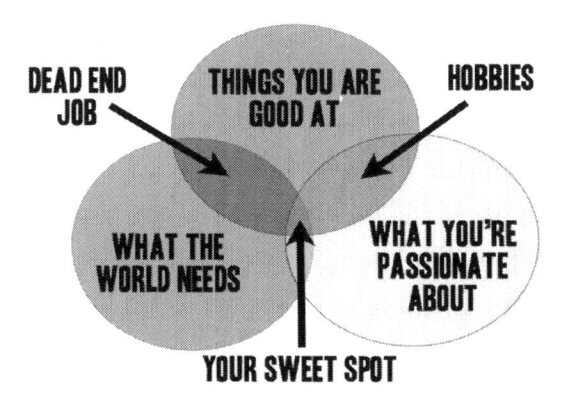

## *Circle One: Things You Are Passionate About*

The first circle will be where you write the things you are passionate about. In this circle are the things that you enjoy or even love doing. An athlete would write their favourite sport (or "sports") in the circle. A musician would put "music." Of course, there could be many other things that someone is passionate about. This could include everything from reading to hiking to hanging out with friends to helping people. Those should be put in circle one as well.

## *Circle Two: Things You Are Good At*

"Jennie, I believe God made me for a purpose, but he also made me fast. And when I run, I feel his pleasure." This is the famous line of Olympic runner, Eric Liddell, in the biographical movie, *Chariots Of Fire*. Liddell was explaining his passion for running to his sister who worried that competitive running was distracting him from missionary work. He assured her that his running was something that pleased God. To Liddell, excelling in his sport was an act of worship God. God gave him the ability to run fast and so he pursued excellence as a gift for God. "Running" is something that Liddell would put in his second circle. This circle is where you put the talents and resources you have been given by God.

Acknowledging what you do well is not bragging, nor is leaving the circle empty an act of humility. Nobody is good at everything: neither is anybody bad at *everything*. What are you good at? For help, you could ask someone who knows you well, like a family member or friend. I am sure they can easily tell you something that you have a talent for. You might not even have realized how good you are at it! We are often hardest on ourselves in the areas where we are the strongest. On the other hand, you might think you are really talented at something when you are actually not. This is why you need feedback from people who love you enough to tell you the truth.

## Circle Three: What the World Needs

In 1865, in a sermon before Queen Victoria, Rev. Charles Kingsley summed up the goal of the third circle. "The age of chivalry is never past, so long as there is a wrong left unaddressed on the earth, or a man or a woman left to say, 'I will redress that wrong or spend my life in the attempt.'" The third circle is where you write the needs of the world that you need to "redress" as Rev. Kingsley put it. You do not put *all* the needs of the world in this circle. There is no circle that could fit them all. You are just going to put the problems of the world that bother you most. These are the ones that keep you up at night; the ones that have you screaming at the TV, "Why doesn't someone do something to stop this?!" These problems can be as local as your own family. My heart aches for people who grow up in broken families, are lonely, or don't get love at home. This is a local problem I would put in my "world needs" circle. Problems that really bother us can also be global. Sex trafficking, third world poverty, and malnutrition are examples of these kinds of world problems. The reason these problems bother you is because they bother God. He wants to do something to stop them and he might want to use you in the process.

Imagine for a moment if every person took on some need in the world and directed all their passions and resources into correcting it. All the circles should be full of insights from your life and observations about the world. Now you must find the place where your passions, talents and the world's needs combine.

## Putting the Circles Together

Where the three circles meet is your sweet spot. If your passions and talents do not fall within the world's needs, this interest could be a hobby for you but it is not a sweet spot. Hobbies are good for weekends, but not for paying bills...unless of course you don't mind sleeping on a friend's couch for the rest of your life.

If you find something the world needs that you are good at but not passionate about, you will end up working in what we might call a dead-end job. Following this vocation will suffocate you if you spend your life doing it. Sometimes a little suffocation is necessary. We have to pay the bills. But if you spend your life in this circle, you will not be following your calling. Your calling will be waiting for you in the sweet spot.

## Case Study #3: A Sweet Spot Applied

I once had a memorable student in my youth group who found where his three circles combined to form his personal sweet spot. His life was never the same from that point on. In the fall of 2007, Cam was a grade twelve student who needed to do a work experience project as a prerequisite to high school graduation. I challenged him not to settle for some mundane mandatory work assignment, but to do something that he was passionate about that would help many people in the process. Cam and his friends came up with the idea to run a citywide campaign to raise money to fight the problem of homelessness in the city of Vancouver, B.C. Needing some help to run a vision of this size, Cam asked me to assist. We called it the *Dollar-A-Day Campaign*.

By taking on something that was "citywide," we needed to take every opportunity to spread the vision of Dollar-A-Day. No one we knew had ever tried anything like this, so it took a great deal of work finding opportunities to promote the cause. We needed some help from Jesus to pull it off.

I love the story found in all four gospels where Jesus feeds five thousand people with a child's fish and bread. It reminds me a lot of our Dollar-A-Day experience. In the story, the disciples came to Jesus with a problem. "Lord, these people have been hanging around with us all day. They are hungry." This is an example of somebody fully aware of his "World's Needs" circle. Jesus' solution to the disciples was simple but a little unrealistic: "Okay, you feed them." The disciples responded pragmatically, "We do not have enough food to give, nor did we bring any money to pay a caterer." Jesus replied, "What do you have? Give it to me." The disciples collected a few loaves and fish, and presented them to the one who would soon be remembered for executing the greatest feeding miracle in history. He took the disciple's offering, blessed it, and fed the multitudes.

Like the disciples, our Dollar-A-Day crew went to Jesus and told him the problem, "Hey Jesus, these people are homeless and they really need your help." We told Jesus about the homeless problem and he told us to do something about it. We said we couldn't due to our personal limitations of people and resources. He said the same thing to us as he said to the disciples some two thousand years ago:

"Give me what you have."

We gave him the best we had and watched him pull off a few miracles. One of those miracles came on a Tuesday night at an inner-city church service where we were serving. In passing, I was told by one of the homeless guys about a citywide Canada Day event about two months away that was being held at Rogers Arena (where the Vancouver Canucks play). Knowing that this could be a good opportunity to promote the campaign, I cold-called the organizer of the event and asked if we could have some time to do an announcement for Dollar-A-Day during the rally. It was a bit of a long shot but she said, "Yes."

What? We were allowed to do an announcement?! I couldn't believe it. After getting a million other requests for stage time, the organizer eventually cancelled all announcements... except one — ours! God had opened a door and we decided to make the most of it. On Canada Day, our team stood on the big stage holding sparklers in front of 11,000 people. We announced our campaign idea that was being run by a grade twelve student and his sidekick youth pastor.

We came up with a plan for after the rally to get as many people as possible to walk two blocks down to Hastings Street and ignite the 7,500 sparklers that we had bought. It was to be a Canada Day celebration in one of the toughest areas of the city.

We had a full band set up waiting for everyone to arrive. Together we belted out "Oh Canada," and "Amazing Grace," and proceeded to worship Jesus in the streets for an hour. Those who counted estimated the number to be around eight hundred Jesus-worshippers that night on Hastings Street. We shut down two, sometimes three, lanes of traffic as we danced and sang with our sparklers. It was a night I will always remember.

I was proud to watch my students use their unique gifts and passions to organize concerts, host fundraisers, lead rallies at their high school, pull all-nighters, and go door-to-door collecting money from friends, family, neighbours and whoever else would contribute. This campaign taught Cam and his team countless leadership and life lessons. Now a decade later, Cam has since married the girl that helped run campaign. He is one of the most successful youth pastors in Metro Vancouver.

The Dollar-A-Day Campaign enjoyed great favour in our city, earning tremendous local and national media coverage, receiving the support of Metro Vancouver churches in several denominations, and providing an experience the students and I will never forget. At the end of the campaign, we earned $40,000 to help local homeless ministries in our city. That is forty thousand more dollars than would have been given should these students have neglected what they were passionate about, what they were good at doing, or what the world of the Downtown Eastside needs.

## To Build or Bury: What are You Doing With Your Talents?

Jesus told this parable to help us evaluate how serious we are about using our talents and passions in an effort to meet the world's needs.

> For it [the kingdom of God] will be like a man going on a journey, who called his servants and entrusted to them his property. To one he gave five talents, to another two, to another one, to each according to his ability. Then he went away. He who had received the five talents went at once and traded with them, and he made five talents more. So also he who had the two talents made two talents more. But he who had received the one talent went and dug in the ground and hid his master's money. Now after a long time the master of those servants came and settled accounts with them. (Matt. 25:14-19)

The first two guys took the talents they were given and did their best with them. When their master returned, he gave them more talents as a reward.

"His master said to him, 'Well done, good and faithful servant. You have been faithful over a little; I will set you over much. Enter into the joy of your master'" (Matt. 25:23).

Nobody who reads this parable wants to be the last guy. He took his talent and put it in the dirt. That's not exciting at all. The parable does not end well for this poor chap.

In this parable Jesus is telling us that how we live this one life God has given us really matters. What you do with your life, your gifts, and your passions - it all counts for something. Not only does it count, but you will be held *accountable by God* for what you do with what you have been given.

James tells us not to be just hearers of the word, but doers as well. It's time to start making decisions and stepping out into what God has called you to (James 1:22). When the master returns and it's time to cash in your talents after a lifetime of pursuing your sweet spot, you will hear those beautiful words,

"Well done good and faithful servant."

## It's Your Turn

It's time to get practical. Take all those ideas and dreams spinning around in your head and get them on paper. I would encourage you to take a piece of paper, find a pen and carve out some time to work through some of the questions I will lead you through below.

1. Think about your primary calling. You are called to have a relationship with Jesus. How is that going? Are you giving your time and effort to see this relationship grow? If this relationship is off, your whole life calling will be off as well. Like a dog chasing its tail, you will spend your time pursuing the wrong things and end up wasting your life.

2. Think about your first circle. What do you love doing most? What kinds of activities get you most excited?

3. Move on to circle number two. What kind of things are you good at? What do people compliment you on? What is it that you could do for hours at a time and not even realize any time had passed at all?

4. In the third circle, write out a few things that you see in the world which really bother you. What moves you emotionally every time you hear about it? How do you think you could use your passions and your gifts to work towards a solution?

5. What ideas come to mind when you combine your three circles? What careers do you think would enable you to work in your sweet spot? Are there any courses you could sign up for or post-secondary courses you could enrol in to help you get where you want to go?

## Conclusion: Become Who You Were Made To Be

My favourite scene in J.R.R Tolkien's classic story, *The Lord Of The Rings* is found in the final book/movie, *The Return Of The King*. It happens in a tent on the evening before a huge battle. Aragorn, an otherwise forgotten Ranger, is called out by Elrond, the king of the elves and his future father-in-law. With Sauron's Orcs launching a final campaign to destroy the realm of men on Middle-earth, a new king is needed to lead the campaign against them. Aragorn is given a sword called Anduril. It is a special sword that cut the ring from Sauron's finger, stripping the evil lord of his power. Growing in strength every day, Sauron's long awaited counter-attack is looming. Legend says that the sword will not be forged again until it can be given to the king of Gondor. In this scene, Elrond anoints Aragorn as that long-awaited king. who will be the one to lead Middle-earth to a much needed victory. Aragorn is told to forsake his obscure Ranger life in favour of his new calling. Elrond charges the future king with these words:

> The man who can wield the power of this sword can summon to him an army more deadly than any that walks this earth. Put aside the ranger. Become who you were born to be.

Aragorn receives the sword and chooses to fight evil, walking in his new identity.

Though I have encouraged you to seek the counsel of friends and family when you are considering what your calling is, in the end you will have to make your own decisions. No doubt other people have all sorts of ideas about your calling in life. Loved ones and strangers alike will suggest you pursue all sorts of things. Some will likely encourage you and some may deeply hurt you. But neither the praises nor the criticisms should define who you are.

That is between you and God. If you are a Christian, your identity is secure no matter what you do. You will always be loved. You will always be saved. Your decision will just be a matter of what you do with all those gifts and all the time you have. No one else will be accountable for this but you.

Spend the rest of your life getting to know your Caller and your calling. Aragorn was called to be a king. What are you called to do? Where do your passions and talents line up with the world's needs? That sweet spot is where you should start.

That is what you are called to become.

LIFE HACK #5
# ALWAYS BE READY

A police officer once visited a Christian private school in his area. He took a few minutes to talk with the class about his favourite Bible story: Joshua and the walls of Jericho.

"Class, who can tell me who knocked down the walls of Jericho?" the policeman asked.

Except for the ticking of the clock on the wall, there was only awkward silence in the room.

One brave girl finally raised her hand and said, "Sir, I do not know who did it but I promise it wasn't me!"

The officer was slightly alarmed that no students knew about Joshua and the walls of Jericho. He found the teacher in the hallway and pulled him aside.

"I was concerned today when none of your students knew who knocked down the walls of Jericho."

"Well, this is terrible," the teacher answered. "Sir, I promise you that I will go back in there and find out who did this terrible thing. Once I find out which one of them is responsible for those broken walls, I will get back to you right away."

The policeman shook his head and headed to see the school principal. He found the school principal and got right down to business. He told her about the students and the teacher, and wondered how that kind of ignorance could be acceptable here.

"You are absolutely right. I promise you that I will deal with this issue immediately," the principal replied.

The officer left the school feeling satisfied that something was going to be done. Two weeks later, the officer got a letter from the school board. It read:

"Dear Constable,
Please accept our formal apology for the state of the walls of Jericho. We take full responsibility for any damage and ask that you send us the bill once they are repaired.
Sincerely,
The School Board."

Thankfully, this is a fictitious story. However, having spoken at many Christian schools, I am ashamed to say that the officer's experience was *inspired* by a true story. If the above cartoon is the kind of experience an officer can get while visiting a Christian school, imagine the response he would get on a secular campus. Today's high schools and universities are some of the most hostile places for a person to profess to be a Christian.

There is a war being fought today between truth and lies. The battle lines are drawn in every class taught in every school, in every piece of legislation being signed at every level of government. Truth and lies are being fought over around every water cooler and every desk in every office, around every sports team, and at every table in every coffee shop. It is a battle we must be aware of and prepared for. If you are a follower of Jesus, you will be engaged in this battle for the rest of your life. Prepare your heart accordingly.

This life hack is meant to encourage us all to study Christian apologetics. I frankly wish that someone had told me about this often uncelebrated aspect of Christian discipleship. I grew up in the church and went through four years of Bible School training before any one told me of the faith-affirming resources that were available to us as Christ-followers.

It was while I was working as a youth and young adult pastor that I entered into a season of doubt in my faith. My responsibility was reaching unchurched high school and university students. They came to my church and they came with their questions:

- How could God be good if there is so much evil in the Bible?
- Why do we trust the Bible? Isn't it full of mistakes and old myths?
- What proof do you have that God is even real?
- How can Christians be so arrogant as to claim that Jesus is the only way to God?

I confess now that these are amazing questions. They show interest and a refreshing depth of thought about the truly important questions of life. My students were asking these questions and, as their pastor, I had no answers for them. Their questions slowly became my doubts. With the rise of the New Atheism movement and the easy circulation of skeptic ideas on Youtube, I found an abundance of reasons to convince me that Christianity must be false. Because I was working as a pastor, was trained only as a pastor, and was considering my only future career calling as a pastor, my whole world was shaken.

During that time, I wasn't as vocal about my faith anymore. I was shy about letting people know that I was a Christian pastor. My confidence eroded and I couldn't shake the thought that maybe I had built my whole life on a lie.

That was many years ago now. Thankfully, God opened my world to a treasure trove of resources that led me through my doubts to a strengthened confidence that Christianity is indeed true. I can see with clarity today that my doubts were actually an invitation to grow as a disciple of Jesus. God wanted to show me just how much there was to learn about the truth of Christianity. I needed to learn to love God with all my *mind*. I needed to feel what honest doubt felt like. I needed to be able to understand the skeptic and some of the roadblocks to faith in Jesus that so many today feel. Finally, I needed to include this Life Hack as a catalyst to help out others who might be facing similar doubts.

Today, I can say with full assurance that I am a Christian because Christianity is true. I am not ashamed to say it and I will engage with anyone about it.

## The Battleground of the Modern University Campus

Those most interested in this chapter will probably be around college or university age. That is the season of life when we seem to experience the most pushback for our beliefs. Even if you are not in university, you need to be ready for attacks on your faith. These may come at a construction site, in an office, or in a dressing room. Attacks can come from anywhere. However, I am using the university experience as my main example because many students will give up on following Jesus before they complete their university degree. Freshman students often show up at university with their virginity, their dreams, and their Christian faith intact. Four years later they graduate with none of the three.

Nancy Pearcey, notes this troubling trend:

> It's a familiar but tragic story that devout young people, raised in Christian homes, head off to college and abandon their faith. Why is

this pattern so common? Largely because young believers have not been taught how to develop a Biblical worldview. Instead, Christianity has been restricted to a specialized area of religious belief and personal devotion.[33]

Most Christian students graduating from high school are shocked when they encounter the open hostility and opposition that awaits them at college or university. While secular universities claim to be centres of tolerance and openness to a plethora of ideas, such campuses are often the most intolerant of Christianity. One atheist writer and university professor, Daniel Dennett says,

> [Students] will see me as just another liberal professor trying to cajole them out of some of their convictions, and they are dead right about that—that's what I am and that's exactly what I am trying to do.[34]

The moment you set foot on a secular university campus, you will find the Christian faith under direct intentional assault from peers, professors, and dead philosophers whose ideas still live on. It is common to hear on university grounds a collective scoffing at the fact that someone today could still believe the Bible to be historically accurate, culturally relevant, and personally applicable.

## Off-Campus Problems

Those of us who are out of post-secondary need to sit back and think that we are outside of the pressure of anti-Christian influences and influencers. If you are a faithful, committed Christian, you will find yourself in spiritual and sometimes confrontational conversations at work, while visiting with friends over coffee, around the dinner table at home (especially if you have teenagers), and even while attending a wedding. I include a wedding because I vividly recall a wedding I was at when a young guy in his twenties who was sitting beside me found out I was a pastor. He proceeded to unload his bazooka of problems with Jesus, the

---

[33] Pearcey, Nancy. *Total Truth: Liberating Christianity From Its Cultural Captivity*. (Wheaton: Crossway, 2005). P. 19.

[34] Dennett, Daniel. *Breaking The Spell: Religion as a Natural Phenomenon*. (New York, NY.: Viking Press, 2006). P. 53.

Bible, and Christians on me. I insisted that a wedding dinner was not the best place for such a conversation and that I would gladly meet him for coffee at another date. He insisted on pushing me and demanding I give an answer for suffering, the Crusades, the destruction of the Canaanites, etc. Thankfully, during the speeches he had no choice but to keep quiet and grant the rest of us at the table some peace. It just goes to show that opposition for being a Christian does not just come at school— it can even come at a wedding.

## My Anti-Bullying Campaign

In an age when people are always looking to prevent bullying, I have observed that Christian students today experience both an implicit and explicit hostility against their beliefs and values. This constitutes religious bullying. It is ironic that our present "age of tolerance" does not have any room for tolerance of the Christian worldview.

I have personally worked hard at becoming an equipped defender of the Christian faith. Maybe it's my hero complex that drives me. Every man wants to be a hero in some way. I strive to protect people's faith in Jesus. Across campuses and at workplaces all over the world today, bullies mock and intimidate my Christian brothers and sisters. These bullies try to silence or scare Christians out of their beliefs and convictions. Intellectual bullies may not harm the body but they can do immense damage to a person's spirit. To combat this kind of attack, we need to raise up men and women who have courage and are trained in defending Christian beliefs.

In order to retain students, church youth groups must compete with the entertainment offered by modern culture — video games, sitcoms, sports and whatever else fills the atmosphere on any given night. Sadly, many youth groups try to compensate and become watered down entertainment shows instead of safe forums for discussing the difficult philosophical questions that Jesus has to offer.

It is not too late, however, to be trained and ready for battle. In his book, *The Weight of Glory*, C.S. Lewis issued a challenge to build our defences and sharpen up on our "reasons for the hope we have in Christ.":

To be ignorant and simple now — not to be able to meet the enemies on their ground — would be to throw down our weapons, and to betray our uneducated brethren who have, under God, no defense but us against the intellectual attacks of the heathen. *Good philosophy must exist, if for no other reason, because bad philosophy needs to be answered.*[35]

You may consider yourself a committed Christian, but that will be of little help in university if you do not understand the reasons for your faith. A well-examined belief system is needed to protect you from the kind of attacks awaiting you on campus. No matter how noble his family is or how much he can bench press, if a knight neglects to put on his armour before battle, he is vulnerable and will be easy to take out.

Some kind of philosophy undergirds every movie, commercial, lecture, or book. Everything we take into our minds is trying to teach us something about how we should think the world is. As Lewis warns us, there is great deal of bad philosophy coming our way. If we do not have good philosophy to counter it, we will be just like that knight without armour.

## Not a New Problem

Jesus often warned his disciples that they should not expect to be treated better than he was treated. Jesus was sent to die on a cross and his followers should expect no better. He promised us, "In this world you will have trouble..." (John 16:33).

In the first century, when the early church was suffering persecution, God raised up a pastor to help those who were struggling. Peter was a well known disciple of Jesus who led a church in Jerusalem. His congregation was full of people who being excluded, mocked, and even killed for their identification with Jesus. In a letter to them, Pastor Peter assured the faithful that their suffering for Jesus' sake should not be a surprise and was not without a good purpose. He wrote this to comfort them:

> Beloved, do not be surprised at the fiery trial when it comes upon you to test you, as though something strange were happening to you.

---

[35] Lewis, C.S. *The Weight of Glory*. (Harper Collins, New York, 1949) p. 50. My italics.

> But rejoice insofar as you share Christ's sufferings, that you may also rejoice and be glad when his glory is revealed. If you are insulted for the name of Christ, you are blessed, because the Spirit of glory and of God rests upon you. (1 Pet. 4:12-14)

## Why You Shouldn't Give Up

Peter sounds the warning but also promises the reward. Too many Christians miss both. Surprised by the pressure that comes from being aligned with Jesus, they deny what they know is true (Jesus), they deny who they have professed to be (followers of Jesus) and they make a short term decision that negates the long term benefits of knowing Jesus (our future hope and glory when he is revealed).

Peter of all people knew what it meant to be surprised by persecution. In Jesus' darkest hour, Peter was ashamed to be seen with him, even denying his association with Jesus to a little girl. Jesus gave Peter a second chance and Peter would go on to face more than his fair share of opposition for being a Christ-follower (he would eventually be crucified like Jesus). As a pastor, Peter was aware that when Christians suffer publicly, others might notice something is different about them. They suffer with dignity. They suffer with courage. They suffer with hope.

Such strength might spark curiosity in others. They ask:

- "Why don't you just deny Christ and live in peace?"
- "Why not just do what everyone else is doing?"
- "How can you have hope in an age of so much despair?"

Peter counsels those who find themselves in such situations:

> In your hearts honour Christ the Lord as holy, always being prepared to make a defense to anyone who asks you for a reason for the hope that is in you; yet do it with gentleness and respect. (1 Pet. 3:15)

1 Peter 3:15 is where we get the term "Apologetics." Apologia is the Greek word for "defense". It is the word used to describe somebody who has to back up a claim that they make. Christians make all sorts of claims like:

- "God is real."
- "God is good"
- "Jesus is the only way to God."
- "The Bible is the true, inspired word of God."

Not everyone believes these statements. According to Peter, those who hold these beliefs must be prepared to back them up with reasons why they are true. That is apologetics. Doing a good job of explaining these reasons is a life hack that will help you immensely in several areas of your life. We will talk more about that in a bit.

Dr. William Lane Craig calls Christian apologetics, "that branch of Christian theology which seeks to provide a rational justification for the truth claims of the Christian faith."[36] Making a defense of your faith is not an aggressive, confrontational effort to win arguments. It is the charitable act of giving reasons for why we believe in Jesus and suffer for him as we do. Apologetics is also an act of loving people in order that they too may experience the hope we have found in Jesus. Peter's hope is that Jesus' church, and Christians everywhere, may live their lives confidently, knowing what they believe, why they believe it, and how to share that belief with others effectively.

## The Art and Science of Christian Apologetics

Apologetics is both a science and an art. It is a science because it deals with the truth found within the various disciplines of knowledge—philosophy, biology, physics, math, and history. It is also an art because each person has the flexibility to craft their arguments however they wish. Some people, like William Lane Craig, use pure logic with watertight syllogisms in their defence of Christianity.

I hardly ever use them. Instead, I use cartoons, stories and jokes to help people understand the rationality of Christianity. Apologists are artists. They can do that kind of thing.

---

[36] Craig, William Lane. *Reasonable Faith*. (Wheaton, Ill.: Crossway Books, 2008). P. 15.

Throughout the history of the church courageous men and women have defended the Christian faith from its many attacks. In Acts 17, Paul is seen giving reasons for his hope in Jesus Christ as Messiah both in Jewish synagogues and through dialogue with the Stoic philosophers of his day. The early church fathers, such as Justin Martyr, Polycarp, Irenaeus of Lyons, Clement of Alexandria, Tertullian, and others, were apologists who served to give the early Christian movement an intellectual undergirding. Several were martyred because of their apologetics. They were followed by some of the greatest minds in history such as: Augustine, Ambrose, Anselm, Thomas Aquinas, John Calvin, and Blaise Pascal (to name a few). Of each of these it could be said, as it was said of King David, he died only, "after he had served the purpose of God in his own generation" (Acts 13:36).

Such is the legacy left to us from church history. Though the Christian faith has never been without attacks against it, it has also never been without a strong defence, thanks to the defenders mentioned above and countless others who have boldly proclaimed the reasons why Christianity, and the Christ it reveals, is worthy of our allegiance.

## The Benefits of Becoming a Defender

There is a military slogan that says, "The more you sweat in training, the less you bleed on the battlefield." This means that there will be work needed on your part. You will need to read books written on Christian apologetics[37] Training requires investment, resources and work. This might even cost you some money. A strong nation has its own defence budget. But you will benefit immensely from the investment you put in. Here are four of the best reasons for spending time and effort pursuing this life hack:

### 1. *You will sharpen your thinking.*

The brain is like a muscle. It needs to be exercised to grow. God gave you a mind, the most complex organism in the entire universe. Your mind is what separates you from the beasts. In studying apologetics, you will be learning what Jesus meant when he taught us to love God with all our minds (Matt. 22:37). Your critical thinking skills will grow as you learn to

---

[37] I have provided a list at the end of this chapter.

create sound arguments and refute bad ones. This exercise of your mind will also benefit you in other areas of life, such as school, work or in parenting. But there's an even greater reason for pursuing this life hack.

## 2. You will honour God.

Saying to God, "I want to learn more about you and learn to respond when people slander your name," is honourable. The results will be wonderful for your growth as a Christian. No longer living on "I hope this is actually true," you will be able to give solid, intellectual reasons for why you have hope in Jesus. Your sharing of these reasons will help to bring about God's kingdom on earth.

## 3. You will grow to appreciate Jesus.

Consider this verse in Philemon 6. Paul writes out his prayer: "and I pray that the sharing of your faith may become effective for the full knowledge of every good thing that is in us for the sake of Christ." Did you catch that? The sharing of our faith leads to more knowledge of the goodness that we have in Jesus. Want to know more about Jesus? It's clear: share your faith with someone. Want to be more confident in sharing your faith? Study Christian apologetics.

## 4. You will be a gift to others

I enjoy helping others. I'm sure you do too. It takes work but it always brings me joy to serve people in whatever way I can. Serving does not just mean paying for their coffee, opening doors or mowing their lawn. You can serve people spiritually too. Jesus said that knowing the truth sets us free. (John 8:32). Understanding apologetics will enable you to show how Christianity is not only a reasonable worldview to hold, but that it is a worldview that will set people free. As a bonus, you will find you are not intellectually bullied anymore and you won't get mad at people for believing differently from you. People get angry when they are threatened. If you study apologetics, your worldview will not feel threatened anymore. Instead, you will find yourself feeling bad for people that buy into so many lies. In my experience, knowledge frees us up to love people. As the Bible says in Jude 22, "have compassion on those who are doubting."

We don't all have to write books on apologetics, but we do all have to give an *apologia*.

## Conclusion

I love sunny fall days when I can rake the leaves in my yard. It is quiet, peaceful and causes little strain on my body. I do not like digging holes nearly as much. Digging takes a lot more work, sweat and toil, and it's hard on my back. Rakes are easier than shovels. However, with shovels, you can discover so much more. In this chapter I have asked you to dig. I want you to not be satisfied with merely raking the surface truths of Christianity. I want you to be able to go deep. Deep is where you find the valuable minerals: diamonds and gold. Deep is where you find truth that endures. Going deep is what makes you strong.

This Life Hack is a challenge to become the kind of person who will not falter in their convictions. Christianity has stood the test of time against its many critics. Will you be the kind who will stand or will you be another casualty who did not make it because you were not prepared?

## Recommended Apologetics Resources

Morrison, Jon. *Clear Minds & Dirty Feet*. (Abbotsford, BC, Apologetics Canada Publishing, 2013.)

Koukl, Greg. *Tactics: A Game Plan for Discussing Your Christian Convictions*, (Grand Rapids, MI: Zondervan, 2008).

Keller, Tim. *The Reason for God: Belief in an Age of Skepticism*. (New York, NY, Penguin Group, 2008).

Budziszewski, J. *How to Stay Christian in College* (Colorado Springs, CO.: NavPress, 2004).

Craig, Wiliam Lane. *On Guard*, (Colorado Springs, Co.: David C. Cook, 2010).

# LIFE HACK #6
# PICK YOUR FRIENDS WISELY

One spring I decided it was time to cross a few things off my Bucket List.[38] I had already tried bungee jumping. The next thing on the list was skydiving.

For some weird reason I thought my life would be better-lived if I jumped out of a plane. I booked an appointment and drove to the site in Abbotsford, B.C. I was greeted, trained and given a tight bright purple jumpsuit that made me look like *Tinky Winky* from the old show, *Teletubbies*. I could have felt emasculated in that bright purple suit, but I compensated for it with the fact that jumping out of a plane was manly regardless of what I was wearing.

After spending a short amount of time in pre-jump training, I made the fated walk to the plane and climbed in. It was the smallest plane I had ever been in.

The door closed and we took off. There was no going back now. The people of Abbotsford were going to see Tinky Winky falling from the

---

[38] This could also be known as the "Things to do before I die" list.

Life Hacks

sky! I watched the automated gauge show our height climbing from 1000 feet to 3000 feet. It increased incrementally until we finally reached the goal of 12,000 feet. From that height, it is amazing to see everything below on such a small scale. My pleasant moment to take in the view came to an abrupt halt when the door slid open and I remembered why I was in this very small plane in the first place. I was jumping out of it.

The pilot looked back and said, "Okay, out you go."

It was gut check time. I had talked about jumping. I had even blogged about it. I had paid for it, written my will, put on the Tinky Winky suit, and gotten into the plane — now it was time to man up and make the jump.

As I write this, my stomach reminds me of how I felt that day. Nauseous. Nervous. Scared. Jelly-legged... and then out I went. Immediately I started falling. No surprise there, I suppose.

The rush of free falling was unlike anything I had ever felt before. I was familiar with being in planes and I was familiar with being on the ground. What was foreign to me was the space in between the ground and the plane. The familiar ground was getting closer with every moment. What state I'd be in when I reached it was the question now in my mind. Up until that moment, my thoughts had been focused entirely on getting out of the plane. I had never thought much about whether or not the parachute was packed correctly or what the whole experience would be like if something went wrong. What if...? Never mind. I continued my fall towards the earth. After screaming a little on the outside to match the screaming going on inside, I looked over my shoulder for any sign of support. My hope that day came in the form of...

...a man strapped to my back.

Thankfully, I was not alone at such a volatile time in my life. In the world of recreational skydiving, it would be silly if, on your first jump, they threw you out of a plane to fend entirely for yourself. This was just recreational skydiving, not D-Day. All beginners are required to take their first jumps with an instructor. My instructor was an expert at skydiving, parachute packing and at knowing exactly when it was time to end our free fall and pull the ripcord. Because of his expertise, I landed safely on the ground. Thanks to the man strapped to my back, I am alive and well to tell this story.

What does this story mean to this chapter? There are two ways this lesson can apply when considering the subject matter of this chapter— the friendships in your life.

*Application Option One*: You and your friends are jumping out of planes together attached at the hip. Each of you is busy making all sorts of choices in your life. Many are bad ones (like wearing purple jump suits). When one friend makes a bad choice, it drags both the decision-maker and their friend to the ground (like free-falling out of a small plane). To make matters worse, each of you is completely unaware that the decisions you are making could lead to dangerous consequences that will inevitably end in a metaphorical collision with the ground. Even worse, you each assume the other is in full control of the situation. You and your friend are both trusting that the other knows how to pack a parachute and will eventually pull the release cord. If you have made a poor choice of friends, it is as if you are wearing your school backpack and forgot the one with the parachute back in the plane. This is an example of friendship gone wrong.

*Application Option Two*: You and your friends are jumping out of planes together and you are attached at the hip. The purple jump suits were a mere lapse in an otherwise use of good judgment. In option two, together you have predetermined who is going to be the one responsible for packing the parachute and pulling the cord. Together, you enjoy a pleasant jump out of the plane creating a lifelong skydiving experience that will serve as a fond memory for the rest of your lives. You are able to work together and support each other through the experience. This is an example of a friendship "gone right."

So which application best describes the experiences of you and your friends?

This chapter is about looking at the Life Hack of having friends in your life that are helping you become who God wants you to be. We will look at the value of various kinds of friendships and how they influence the person you are becoming.

I have included this chapter because there is not much out there on the subject of friendship. People don't seem to be talking about it. I see a lot of people *having* friends and *valuing* friends. We are just not thinking much about why we do it and what kind of effect our friendships have on us. Good friendships, however, are a life hack worth talking about. Let me explain why I believe this is so.

## We Need Each Other

Friendships are an important part of being human. Research shows that they are on the decline. That is, people are getting lonelier every day because they lack friends. Robert Putnam observed this and wrote a commentary on our modern society that he called *Bowling Alone*.[39] Putnam observed that Americans (and Canadians) are becoming increasingly disconnected from each other in families, neighbourhoods, churches, schools, etc. The statistics show that we belong to fewer organizations and clubs; we know our neighbours less well, and hang out with our friends and family members less frequently. As Putnam's title suggests, we are also bowling alone more often. Interestingly enough, modern Americans are bowling more than ever before, but they are not bowling in groups. They are just bowling alone. Who bowls alone? Maybe it's just me, but isn't the best part of bowling the frequent high-fives? Because people are bowling in isolation, even the high-five is on the decline. Putnam traces how changes in work, family structure, television, computer technology, suburban life, gender roles (e.g. women's roles in society), and other factors have all contributed to this decline and the subsequent loneliness epidemic.

When she was alive, Mother Teresa observed that the greatest problem in this world is not starvation— it's loneliness. That is a profound statement given that it came from a woman who devoted her life to working with the world's most destitute in Calcutta, India.

Loneliness is a global problem. There is a unique newspaper in the UK called *The Big Issue*. Copies of it are sold by homeless men and women all over the country in an effort to fight homelessness. In one issue that focused on loneliness in English culture, the writer made a profound observation. He noted that most people's image of loneliness is that of

---

[39] Putnam, Robert. *Bowling Alone*. (Simon and Schuster, 2000).

an old lady sitting alone in her apartment. The truth is that the picture of loneliness in our culture today could just as well be a well-dressed man trying desperately to make conversation with a girl standing next to him in a bar. What an interesting point. These days we can be surrounded by people both in person and on social networking and yet still feel totally alone.

We need relationships. God made us that way. We are negatively affected by our lack of relationships. We are also affected by the relationships we do have.

Consider what Ecclesiastes 4:9-10 says about the impact relationships can make in our lives.

> Two are better than one, because they have a good reward for their toil. For if they fall, one will lift up his fellow. But woe to him who is alone when he falls and has not another to lift him up!

This passage is not meant to be read solely at weddings. It is about the powerful potential of all relationships.

Your friends can be one of your greatest strengths. They can make you a better person. In Ephesians 6, Paul tells the people at the church of Ephesus to approach life as a spiritual battle, and to be armed with the full armour of God: the helmet, breastplate, belt, shield, shoes, and sword. In the original Greek translation, the imperative of "put on" is written in the second person plural. This indicates that Paul was giving a command, not to individuals, but to groups of two or more. He is saying they are to arm themselves for battle *together*. He is mobilizing an entire community. Personally, I need a community of friends to help me in the battle because, left alone, I can be horrendously unprepared for the challenges of warfare. All too often I can't find my sword, I forget my helmet at home and, instead of battling, I would rather settle for a lazy nap underneath a shady tree. However, with friends fighting beside me, my life is completely different. Friends can be there to kick me out of bed and get me excited for battle. A friend will get my back as I get theirs. This is why we need each other.

On the other hand, a friend could tell you that shields, swords, and helmets are items found in fairy tales, and then pass you some cocaine. It really depends on the kind of friends you have.

## A Proverb Worth Applying

The book of Proverbs is a book about wisdom. Having wisdom is defined as knowing the difference between right and wrong and then choosing to do right. The writer of Proverbs was a wise man named Solomon. In one proverb, Solomon wrote about the importance of choosing your friends wisely. Proverbs 13:20 says, "He who walks with the wise grows wise, but a companion of fools suffers harm." Solomon wants us to know that our friends will help determine the quality and direction of our lives. There is a reason why the Holy Spirit inspired Solomon to include the people we walk with as one of the primary tools we can use to become wise. On the other hand, our friends can also affect us negatively. Consider the warning of Proverbs 22:24-25 "Make no friendship with a man given to anger, nor go with a wrathful man, lest you learn his ways and entangle yourself in a snare."

How are your friends affecting you? Take a moment and ask yourself these questions to see just how influential your friends are in shaping who you are:

> 1. Have I ever made a decision that went against my own personal beliefs and values because my friends pressured me to do so?

> 2. Have I ever compromised on something I knew God didn't want me to do but, because my friends were doing it, I decided to go along with them?

Start thinking about this: are you growing in wisdom by walking with wise people? Or are you becoming foolish by hanging out with fools?

Next time you are hanging out, I recommend taking a good look at the people you call friends. Ask yourself: Do I want to become just like these people? Do I like who they are? Do I like where they are headed?

The answers you formulate will allow you to determine how your friends are influencing you. As sure as the sun will rise tomorrow, the more time you hang out with your friends, the more you will start to look, sound, and behave like them. You will dress like them and talk like them. You will read the books they read, listen to the music they listen to and watch the movies they watch. If they get tattoos, you will probably get tattoos. If they get piercings, it is likely that you, too, will get piercings. (and in the same places). Most importantly, you and your friends will, at the very least, begin to share the same values, which means that you will all be heading in the same direction.

## Three Kinds Of Friendship We All Need

I want to look at the relationships of the Apostle Paul, one of the greatest Christian leaders in all of history. Nobody did more for the sake of the Kingdom of God than Paul. He wrote most of the New Testament, pioneered some of the most dynamic missions movements ever and was relentless despite all kinds of opposition. How was he able to accomplish so much? Certainly Paul had the grace of God, but he also had some dynamic relationships to help him. We will look at three kinds of relationships Paul had.

### *1. Gospel Partners*

"Gospel partners" may be an unfamiliar term for you. I think it is a powerful description of the type of friends Paul had. Because Paul had been called by God to travel around as a missionary, he had to hold his friends lightly. He wrote a letter from prison to some friends in Philippi commending them for their "partnership in the gospel from the first day until now" (Phil. 1:5). Their partnership in the gospel meant a great deal to Paul. The New Testament teaches us that Paul had teamed up with men he trusted who would help him fulfill the call of God on his life.

Paul was always on the move. Jesus gave him beloved allies along the way to strengthen and support him. Look how Paul describes his one friend, Tychicus: "He is a *beloved brother* and *faithful minister* and fellow servant in the Lord" (Col. 4:7). It's not like, "Tychicus, he's a good lead-off hitter for our softball team— I need him around for that." Or, "we went to school together and connect over video games mostly." Instead, Paul says that his friend is a beloved brother, faithful minister and servant of God" with Paul.

Likewise, Paul says of his friend, Epaphroditus: "a servant of Christ Jesus, greets you, always struggling on your behalf in his prayers…he worked hard for you" (Col. 4:12). How was Paul so successful as a leader, preacher, pastor and missionary? He surrounded himself with hard-working, gritty guys like Epaphroditus. Perhaps there is no more shining example of this than when Paul describes how much his friend, Epaphroditus, meant to him.

> I have thought it necessary to send to you Epaphroditus my brother and fellow worker and fellow soldier, and your messenger and minister to my need, for he has been longing for you all and has been distressed because you heard that he was ill. Indeed he was ill, near to death. But God had mercy on him, and not only on him but on me also, lest I should have sorrow upon sorrow (Phil 2:25-27).

Do you have friends like that? Men or women who are so sold out for the mission of God that they would risk their lives to see it fulfilled? The camaraderie that comes from being soldiers (Paul's word, not mine) together is intense and eternal. Gospel partnerships are like line dancing. The gospel is the music that moves people around. The caller is Jesus. He tells us which people should come together and where they should go.

These kinds of friendships are a gift from God. C.S. Lewis wrote a great deal about friendship in his book, *The Four Loves*. It is this lengthy quote that has made me appreciate so much the gospel partnerships that God has brought into my life. I see now that they are a gift by the providence of God.

> In friendship…we think we have chosen our peers. In reality a few years' difference in the dates of our births, a few more miles between certain houses, the choice of one university instead of another…the accident of a topic being raised or not raised at a first meeting--any of these chances might have kept us apart. But, for a Christian, there are, strictly speaking no chances. A secret master of ceremonies has been at work. Christ, who said to the disciples, "Ye have not chosen me, but I have chosen you," can truly say to every group of Christian friends, "Ye have not chosen one another but I have chosen you for one another." The friendship is not a reward for our discriminating and good taste in finding one another out. It

is the instrument by which God reveals to each of us the beauties of others.[40]

## 2. Mentors

The second kind of friendship we all need is the one that gives us encouragement and coaching. You can have this kind of friendship at any age in life. As a new parent, I need a mentor more than I ever did as a teenager. We can assume that the Apostle Paul received some kind of mentoring all through his public and private life. That's how education worked back then. Your teacher was your mentor. He received his formal education under a Jewish mentor named Gamaliel (see Acts 22:3). It is the mentoring he received as a Christian that I want to focus on.

Before becoming the most successful church planter in the history of the world and the writer of most of the New Testament, Paul was a judgmental man who spent his time persecuting Christians. He hated anyone who followed Jesus and wanted nothing more than to see them dead. Amazingly, Paul converted to Christianity when the risen Jesus appeared to him on a road and told him to stop his tirade against Christianity. Having met Jesus personally, Paul was radically transformed and zealously started preaching about his new faith in Jesus to anyone who would listen.

Paul was a new man, but he was still rough around the edges. The book of Acts reports that the other disciples were scared of him, thinking he might revert back to his old ways. He needed someone who would believe in him and teach him a few things about how to be a follower of Jesus. Paul needed this kind of friend.

Along came a man named Barnabas whose name means "son of encouragement." How about that for a name? If I had a friend named "Encouragement," I would probably never leave that friend's side. We would always get invited to parties just because that friend would be so pleasant to be around. As it turns out, Barnabas' character was true to his namesake. Eugene Peterson's *The Message* translates Acts 9:26 as,

---

[40] CS Lewis, *The Four Loves* (Harper Collins, New York, NY, 1960) p.83.

"Barnabas took Paul under his wing."[41] That's a great way of putting it. Barnabas, or Encouragement as we could call him, saw a young man rough around the edges but still full of exciting potential. Barnabas showed Paul around, taught him about Jesus, introduced him to a few people, and probably helped him plan for his future ministry.
We see all throughout the Book of Acts just how much Barnabas and Paul experienced together.

- They were called by God on a mission together (13:1-3).
- They saw God do powerful miracles in their midst (13:6-12, 14:8-10).
- They preached and ministered in various cities (13:13-49).
- They no doubt laughed a lot when people misunderstood them (14:11).
- They suffered together (14:19-28).
- They even got into some heated and public disagreements (15:36-40).

Barnabas had a profound impact on Paul's life, and the two became great friends by going on church planting road trips together. I'm sure if Paul were able to speak to us today, he would tell us with tremendous gratitude about his encouraging friend, Barnabas. He would tell us how Barnabas was willing to be his friend by nurturing his potential and "taking him under his wing."

## The Importance of Mentors

I know what it's like to need to come under someone's wing for shelter. My teenage years were an awkward ordeal. I was introduced to girls, zits, high school, sports, climbing and sliding on the popularity ladder, youth group, puberty, God, doubts, plus a load of crazy and mysterious questions. I definitely had a whole bunch of new experiences to process which would have been really difficult to do alone. I thank God for the men he put in my life. Those guys took an interest in me, deciding that my wellbeing and sanity were worth their time. They believed that I was worth investing themselves in, ensuring that I made it through school alive.

---

[41] Peterson, Eugene. *The Message*. (Colorado Springs, CO. : NavPress, 2000).

My mentors took time to be with me and to listen to my stories. They would offer guidance and wisdom, which have helped me develop into a better man, a better leader, and a better follower of Jesus. These memories are what I remember best about growing up with older men in my life. It was to my benefit to have someone older, with perspective, to talk to when it felt like my dramatic teenage life was falling apart. They were there after all the breakups, the mistakes, the devastating hockey games, and the times when I was on the brink of giving up on Christianity altogether.

I do not remember much of what I was taught in youth group but I do remember these men vividly. I am eternally grateful for the impact they had on my life. Simply said, I am who I am today because of those guys. Today, I continue to seek out older, wiser men who will speak into my life. Everyone needs invaluable mentors like these.

If you do not have a person like this in your life, you need to find one. You need a mentor because life can be difficult and deceiving if you are left entirely on your own. A person who can listen to your experiences and offer godly counsel, as well as tell you about their own experiences, is an awesome gift.[42] Trust me, no one has enough life experience to go it alone. Your friends are neither wise enough nor smart enough to fill this role for you. So how do you find a mentor? It's actually quite simple:

## How To Find a Mentor

First and foremost, you need to pray. Ask God to show you the right person to approach. Secondly, trusting that God is at work in your life, think about the people around you that you admire. It could be anyone who has characteristics that you would like to have passed on to you.

Once you have identified the person you want to learn from, I recommend taking the following steps:

---

[42] I have several mentors for various areas of my life. Some help me with theological issues, some help me with financial decisions, some help me with marriage and family matters. We can learn something from a plurality of sources rather than just having one person as your sole mentor

# Life Hacks

*1. Invite them for lunch.* Most leaders I know need to eat. They do it every day. This means that they will have to take some time out of their busy schedule to sit down and eat. If they are sitting and eating, they might as well be talking to someone. That someone could be you. Inviting someone to lunch is a great way to have their undivided attention for at least thirty minutes to an hour. When you invite them, mention that you would like to take them out and ask three questions. It will make them feel important. You can even send the questions in advance so they have time to prepare their answers.

*2. Ask some prepared questions.* People love to help others. They especially love to help out in an area in which they feel strong. Bring three questions you would like to have answered and use them to guide the conversation.

*3. Pay for their lunch.* You have just gleaned all sorts of useful and invaluable information. The least you can do now is keep up your end of the bargain and pay.

If the experience was beneficial, thank the person for their time and tell them what you have learned. When it is appropriate, you can ask to meet again because you have more questions.

On this approach to finding a mentor, I agree with American Pastor Andy Stanley who says that most people worthy of being a mentor do not feel like they have the time to do a good job of it. They will feel burdened by your request to mentor them (at least for the long-term) and might decline the request if you ask. Most people, however, do not mind taking some time every now and then to help someone else out (especially if it is over lunch and the other person is paying!). Once you meet with the person a few times, you are pretty much being mentored by them. They do not have the burden of mentorship expectation and you are being helped by their life.

Of course, you do not have to do it this way. It is just something I have learned. I have received some amazing opportunities meeting with leaders that I would never have had if I had asked them to "mentor me."

If the only thing you take from this chapter is the mandate to get a mentor, that's a win.

## 3. Mentees

Everyone should have the joy of being a mentee. That is, "a person who is advised, trained, or counselled by a mentor." The third and final type of friendship I am recommending you pursue is the kind where you are encouraging to someone else.. We learned that Paul had help from Barnabas, but he also devoted himself to helping a young leader named Timothy.

Paul took Timothy under his own wing and walked with this younger companion. In fact, Paul wrote two letters to Timothy that were so influential that they were passed around churches, preserved, and exist today in our Bibles as First and Second Timothy.

In these letters, Paul gave Timothy a backstage pass into his own life. He allowed Timothy to see his struggles and hear the story of God's grace in his life, which gave Timothy insight into the very heart of his mission.

Jesus was also mentee to a lunch pail crew of young men we know as his disciples. These guys were to be the ones who would closely follow him for three years. They were the first ones responsible for ensuring that the good news of God's kingdom spread around the world (what a responsibility to give). In Matthew 10:8, Jesus sent out his newly recruited disciples on a short-term mission trip. Before they went, he gave them a pep talk to prepare for the trip. Essentially, Jesus told them it was time to stop receiving only and to start serving: "Freely you have received, now freely give."

If you have been raised in the church, you most likely have been receiving freely without giving all that much. The early days in our church experience is about receiving. Here's how it goes: we attend nursery, move up to Sunday school, move up to youth group, and then graduate. It costs us relatively nothing...and it costs a whole lot of time, energy and discipline by those volunteers and pastors who are responsible for our development.

The saying, "it takes a whole village to raise a child" is certainly true in church. We have likely been "works in progress" for many people. In addition to your parents, there have been teachers, coaches, extended family, friends, friends' parents and community leaders, all helping to shape who you are today. They had a goal that one day you would become a strong contributor to society. A great deal of prayer, energy, sweat and even some blood went into shaping us to ensure this happens.

Freely we have received. Now it is time for us to freely give.

It is time to start pouring yourself into someone else's development. Someone else needs to be taught the lessons you have learned; someone else needs to be warned not to walk down roads that you should have avoided. Someone else needs to talk through their problems with an older friend that they can trust. Someone else needs you.

Imagine who you would be if you'd had no help getting to where you are today. What if there is a person out there that is much like you were when you were a young teenager, who needs you in their life? I can hear some objecting, "But I didn't have anyone there in those darkest moments." Maybe you didn't. How comforting would it have been to have had someone to help you sort through your emotions and problems, or just to make you laugh? How great would it have been to have had someone to let you know they loved you and were praying for you? You can be the someone you never had.

## Someone to Wait in the Rain for You

There is a scene in *Spiderman 2* that inspired me to never underestimate the impact we can make in another person's life. The scene comes just after Peter Parker gives up his superhero alter ego as Spiderman to pursue a normal life away from fighting crime. Of course, there is a girl involved and Peter wants to get to know her without Spiderman getting in the way. Peter's move was understandable; Mary Jane is the type of girl for whom a guy would gladly give up the red and blue pajamas.

While walking home, Peter is approached by a downtrodden neighbourhood kid. The young boy is dragging his feet around because he has just learned that Spiderman is out of the life-saving/crime-solving business. The kid has lost his hero. Aunt May explains to Peter just how devastating this can be.

> Everybody needs a hero, courageous sacrificing people, setting examples for all of us. Everybody loves a hero, people line up for

them, cheer for them, scream their names, and years later tell how they stood in the rain for hours just to get a glimpse of the one who told them to hold on a second longer. I believe there's a hero in all of us, that keeps us honest, gives us strength, makes us noble. And finally gets us to die with pride. Even though sometimes we have to be steady and give up the thing we want most, even our dreams.

Who is going to wait in the rain for you?

Invest yourself in someone else. There are many opportunities to become a hero. You can volunteer to be a youth leader at church, become a big brother, coach a sports team or volunteer at a summer camp.

Freely you have received, now freely give. These friendships will affect the direction and quality of your life.

## The Legacy That Matters Most

Everyone wants to be seen with celebrities. Posting a selfie with someone famous is a pinnacle of modern day achievement. We want to be associated with celebrities. But what kind of lasting impact does being connected with these influencers of society truly have?

The following is an exercise attributed to a wonderful Christian man named Charles Schulz. Schulz was the creator of Charlie Brown and his dog "Snoopy" from the famous *Peanuts* comic strip. While you don't have to actually answer the questions, read through them and you will see just how important our relationships are to us.

1. Name the five wealthiest people in the world.
2. Name ten people who have won the Nobel or Pulitzer Prize.
3. Name the last half dozen Academy Award winners for best actor and actress.
4. Name the last decade's worth of Super Bowl winners.

How did you do? The clear point is that those who are celebrated today are largely forgotten tomorrow. Today's headlines are tomorrow's recycling. Those who won all those awards are literally the best of the best. Their titles are temporary and their trophies are now tarnished. Let's move on to another set of questions:

1. List a few teachers who aided your journey through school.
2. Name three friends who have helped you through a difficult time.
3. Name five people who have taught you something worthwhile.
4. Think of a few people who have made you feel appreciated and special.

Wasn't that so much easier? Charles Schulz was showing us that the people who make the biggest impact in our lives are not the most famous, the richest or those who have the most awards. They are the ones who care the most for us. Whose list will you be on one day?

## Conclusion: Choose Friendship

Choosing God-honouring relationships is a Life Hack because not having them is a death trap. Loneliness is an epidemic in Western culture. God has wired us for relationships with each other. In this chapter we looked at three kinds of friendships that the Apostle Paul had: gospel partners, mentors and mentees. I encouraged you to find friends who will challenge you and bring you closer to Jesus. I also encouraged you to find a mentor to help you navigate the tough roads ahead. Lastly, I encouraged you to return the favour by mentoring someone who needs your help.

The old saying from my childhood is still true: The best way to make a friend is to be a friend. To find and make friends, do things for people that you would appreciate others doing for you. Jesus taught us, "Whatever you wish that others would do to you, do also to them" (Matt. 7:12). With kind words and loving actions you will become a good friend as you "Spur one another on towards love and good deeds" (Heb. 10:24).

You will be better for it. Your friends determine the character and quality of your life. It's just that simple.

We now transition to the far less simple romantic relationships in your life.

LIFE HACK #7
# BECOME THE KIND OF PERSON YOU WOULD LIKE TO MARRY

This is the chapter that the hopeless romantics may skip to first. That's ok. These kinds of relationships are important and extra important to some. Life Hack #7 is intended to ensure we are engaging in the worthwhile pursuit of a spouse with wisdom, and in a way the honours both the opposite gender and the God who first thought of this kind of relationship.

Do not go into this kind of relationship lightly. Be forewarned: the choice of the person you marry is the second most important decision you will make in your life. In this chapter I'd like to share some insights that I have learned from friends, relatives, mentors, books and most importantly, the Bible.

## Who This Chapter Is For

This chapter might not be for everyone. Some people feel called by God to live a life of celibacy. That is an incredibly honourable calling. It is one we do not talk about enough. There are many out there who will never get married. It's more common than we ever talk about. If marriage is not on your radar, you can skip this chapter for sure. Some people might already be married and need not think about preparing to get married. They too can skip ahead. Some readers might have already been married once and do not want to try it again. This chapter might not be for them either.

This chapter is really for those who are married and want to think deeper about it or for anyone would like to be married one day and want to be as prepared as possible for this milestone. This Life Hack is about preparing your heart and your character for the beauty and the challenge that marriage will bring your way.

## A Little More of My Story

I did not get married until I was thirty-two years old. That might not seem like such an advanced age to some people but in "church years" I was an old man. I wanted to get married earlier but I confess that I personally was not mature enough for it. I dated several girls but was not mature enough for the commitment that marriage demands of us men.

When I first met Hayley I was absolutely stunned at just how beautiful, wise, loving and smart she was. I got that from looking at her Facebook profile picture after a friend sent me a link to it. Thinking we would be a fine pair, his goal was to set us up together.

My friend Andy gave a glowing endorsement of his friend, Hayley. He wondered if I'd like to drive across the city to meet her at his church. I willingly obliged. I assumed that when he invited me to come to his church and meet her that he had given her a similar kind of reference about me. That's what matchmakers usually do. They inform both parties about the *existence* and strengths of the other. I guess Andy thought he was fine having done only half the job. Hayley received no such reference about me!

## Become the Kind of Person You Would Like to Marry

When I finally got to meet her after church that day, I couldn't figure out why she was so cold towards me. It was clear that she had no clue who I was nor did she seem too keen to find out. When I asked Andy about it afterward, he informed me that he had never mentioned to her that we were being set up. Driving home that day, I concluded that the ice had been broken, at least, and I would try a little harder the next week.

I would never recommend one-way setups. Thankfully, by God's grace, in my case, it worked.

After some awkward first few encounters, and a few months of dating, I am thankful to report that, in the fall of 2013, I married the girl from the one-way set up. We love each other more each day. I do not like saying that we "fell in love" because love is not something that we stumbled into. We are both intentional Type-A personalities. We build love, nurture love, and work hard at love all so we can enjoy the most love that God intended for marriage. It can be a lot of work at times. But it is so rewarding.[43]

Our five-month engagement alone took plenty of work. Getting married is about talking, planning and preparation. Engagement is like working a part-time job on top of whatever else you are doing already (This is stereotypically true for the girl, but men are getting more involved these days in the planning process). The budget, venues, guest list, invitations, outfits, decorations, and all the other things that go into a wedding ceremony and reception demand a lot from the couple and their families. There is much work to do before anyone is ready to walk down the aisle.

Most of the work in my marriage came long before I met Hayley. Getting married in my thirties, I had time to think about what kind of girl I felt would be best for me. I also had ample time to make sure I was the kind of person that was marriage material. That's the kind of preparation I want to help you with. Think of this chapter as your pre-pre-marital counselling. A pastor/counsellor/mentor can only cover so much in the five or so sessions that you meet before wedding day. There is much work prior to that. Here's the Life Hack of doing the hard work beforehand.

---

[43] For more on this, check out chapter 5 of Matt Walsh's book, *The Unholy Trinity* (Crown Pbl, New York, NY. 2017). Pages 85-100.

## Preparing for Marriage—Not Just a Wedding

Though the wedding is important, more work needs to be done during the engagement stage than just wedding planning. Many people get so caught up in planning a wedding that they neglect to prepare for their marriage. What kind of person are you going to be as you either walk down the aisle or stand smiling at the altar waiting for your bride to come to you? It's important to make sure you are preparing for this adventure that awaits you.

Married people will tell you that, though marriage is the best and most beautiful relationship two people can enjoy, it is also one of the most difficult. "But it seems so wonderful all the time in movies and books!" That's right, it does. And remember that most of the writers of those movies and books were divorced. Writing, reading, talking and dreaming about marriage is easy. Actually living out a God-honouring marriage is the challenge.

We know marriage is difficult because even Nelson Mandela, who served as South African president from 1994–1999, went through a divorce. The man endured twenty-seven years of prison and persevered through horrific, dehumanizing conditions in South Africa. After being released, he spent only six months with his wife before he broke.

"I can't take this anymore!!!"

Nobody ever wants to end up divorced. On their wedding day no one stares across at their beloved and vows, "I promise to start our marriage off well, but then I'm most likely going to get bored with this relationship, and possibly have an affair that will leave me broke, you heartbroken, and the children forever wounded. My poor decisions will result in a deep guilt and hurt that may continue on through several generations. Oh and by the way... I do."

I read this on a Starbucks cup: "You will only be as happy as the least happy person in your marriage." That's the way I see it too. Are you a miserable person who thinks that getting married is going to make you happy? I don't think it will. Just as fame, money and nicer cars don't make you happy, simply getting married won't make you happy either.

Today is the day to start preparing for the most sacred and intimate relationship that you will ever be a part of, should this be in God's plan for you. Before you say, "I do," you can save yourself a lot of pain by getting a few things in order in your own life.

Pastor Tim Keller suggests that before you answer the question, "Who is the one for me?" you need to first answer the question, "Who am I?" That's what this book has been all about and will be a major focus of this chapter.

I would like to help you prepare for marriage as well as I can. Before you can marry (in our culture) you are probably going to date. That is a process worth talking about on its own.

## The Dating Process

Dating may not be the best system out there, but my guess is that it will be the one you use when it comes to finding the right mate for you. That's what dating is for: mate selection. If you are not thinking about the possibility of marrying someone, you are not ready to date yet. I've heard it said that dating with no intent to marry is like going to the grocery store with no money. You either leave unsatisfied or you take something that is not yours.

If you are going to be an active dater, you have to accept the high level of emotional turmoil that you will incur. When dating, you are essentially taking your heart, the most intimate and vulnerable part of who you are, in an open hand, holding it out to another person and essentially saying:

"Here you go; do what you want with this."

I advise all involved in this venture to proceed with caution. Sometimes the recipient will take your heart and trample it; sometimes your attempts will be received and cherished. In the early stages, it is hard to determine which way it will go. This is why dating is only for the courageous, for the ones who are willing to risk hurting or being hurt.

Some people marry the first person they ever date. Most of us, before having our hearts cherished, will have a few experiences with our hearts being broken. That is why we call it "heartbreaking" when a relationship does not work out. It really hurts when something is broken; broken things need to be healed before they can become whole again. The most fragile things in the world often take the longest to heal. This is why Proverbs says, "Above all else, guard your heart, for it is the wellspring of life" (Proverbs 4:23).

The question could be asked: why bother with all the risk?

## Marriage Is a Good, God Thing

Humans throughout history have been intrigued by the idea of love and have always had the desire to be in it. It is a beautiful gift to share committed life-long love with another person. That's why people do it so often. That's why we write songs and poems, and make movies about love. That's why, even with all the bad press marriage receives, weddings go on all the time. Love and marriage are good things; and yes, they are God things.

Our desire to love someone and be loved in return comes from God. We are made in the image of a God who loves passionately. He put a capacity to love inside us. Marriage was God's idea. The Bible starts with the wedding of Adam and Eve in the early pages of Genesis and it ends with a wedding as Jesus unites with his church in the final chapter of Revelation.

The first wedding occurs after the creation of the world. Following each day of creation, God proclaimed that everything was good, but in the case of humanity on the sixth day, he went one step further and called us humans, "very good" (Gen 1:31).

With all God's creating and proclaiming in those early days, there was one thing in creation that God called "not good." It was not good for a man, in this case *Adam*, to be all by himself (Gen. 2:18). Be assured, it was not fatal for Adam to be alone, it was just "not good." He needed some help. Without Eve, we can only imagine all the terrible fashion combinations he would have worn as he walked out of his tent day after day. Let's not even mention the hygiene issue. God gave Eve to Adam, and here's how the first recorded marriage went.

## The First Wedding

After God declared that Adam was lonely on his own, he put his man into a deep sleep and mysteriously made Eve out one of his ribs. God didn't take from Adam's front (so that he would be chasing Eve forever), nor did he take her from behind (as to always have her following him). God formed Eve from Adam's side so that the two could be complementary companions. God brought Eve, now the pinnacle of all of God's creation, to Adam in Genesis 2:22. In essence God said, "Okay, I got the kinks out with that first one...less hair this time. A little cleaner and a bit better smelling."

Eve was presented to Adam and the two were joined together by God. It was the first wedding. In the Bible, when two people become married, it says that under God they become "one flesh" (Gen. 2:24). That's what happens when a man and woman pair up; the two individuals join to become one.

The "two-made-one" complemented each other as God created them to do. Adam brought his God-given masculinity to Eve. Eve brought her God-given femininity to Adam. They were naked and not ashamed of who they were. They shared their life together. They talked with God together. They were two distinct people but mysteriously they were one.

If only it had remained that way. Sin came along in Genesis 3 and messed up everything. When it comes to its effect on our relationships, sin has instant results. Adam hid from Eve and blamed her for his folly. They no longer trusted each other. They sewed fig leaves together to hide themselves from each other.

Divorce is one example of how sin tries to divide the unity that God creates — two people who came together try to split up to make two again. If you have ever glued two pieces of construction paper together, let them dry and then tried to take them apart again, you will know that they can never be as they were originally. Broken marriages are an epidemic in our world today because, as Romans 6:23, teaches us, the wages of sin is death. Thankfully, sin does not always lead to death if we let Jesus take care of things. Jesus died the death we deserve, taking death in our place. Instead of leading to death, if Jesus is at the centre of a relationship, sin can lead to the cross of Jesus. This cross is the key to our reconciliation with God and with each other. The gospel ensures we have long-lasting, Christ-centred relationships/marriages because it does not allow sin to remain at the centre of our most important relationships.

Ever since that very first wedding, God has been bringing sons and daughters of Adam and Eve together as one. We have already established that God gave the desire to share your life with someone. At the right time, you will most likely get married. Before you enjoy spending the rest of your life married to someone, there is another great gift that you can enjoy right away:

Being single.

## What to Do Until Then

Single? "But what if I end up as a lonely spinster with blue hair and thirty-six cats?" you might ask. I suppose that it could happen. If you are under twenty-five, already own three cats, and your phone is full of pictures of felines, I can give no guarantees you won't end up with more cats. I warn you, this could be a deterrent to wooing a future spouse. But I encourage others with this one statistic: 93% of people will get married at some point. I don't have a good source for this number, but I heard it somewhere and it sounds about right. I think that the vast majority of people who want to be married, end up married. Granted, it doesn't always happen on the timeline they would like, but they get there eventually.

Let's talk a bit about what happens when those natural desires for connection with the opposite sex go wild. When your desires mix with sin and our crazy culture, we start to pursue good relationships for bad reasons.

## A Few Humble Words for the Girls (From a Guy)

Girls, I don't claim to understand the female psyche, but I have observed that you are very relational beings. You thrive when your relationships are going well and stumble when they are suffering. Like gas in a car, relationships can be your fuel. God made you for vibrant relationships with both guys and girls. As a guy, I appreciate the value women place on connecting with people and I respect their desire for intimacy. The world needs more of that. Guys need to learn to value this aspect of women much more than we do. One of the many reasons God has placed the female gender in our lives is to remind us that, in the end, our relationships are really what matter most.

Girls love relationships so much they will devote entire conversations to talking about all the people in their world that are in relationships (even if it means talking so loudly about all their relationships that it disturbs all the other people sitting near them in the coffee shop trying to write chapters on relationships… but I digress.).

What I do not like is when I hear girls talk about their need to be in a romantic relationship *all the time* as if that is all that matters. I have a problem when girls feel they are only valuable or worthwhile if they are in a romantic relationship. Some girls have believed the lie that if they "just had a boyfriend" then life's problems would disappear and they would finally be able to graduate from the proletariat "single" class of women to the bourgeoisie "in a relationship" class.

Perhaps this is just my own experience but, as a guy, I have noticed that I seem to have caused more problems in relationships than I have actually solved. If Hayley had thought I would show up and solve all her problems, she would soon have realized that, being married to me, she would be in for one disappointment after another. I know many guy friends who are the same in this regard. We may be able to solve some problems by keeping our wives warm, opening jars, fighting off robbers, paying for dinner and participating in the creation of children, but we also create a bunch more problems.

I know that does not sound very romantic, but it does sound true. Guys do not solve all your problems. You may need to learn this on your own. For now, just be warned.

I would hate to see you constantly disappointed because you found out the hard way that a man you thought would be your personal saviour turns out to be an imperfect, selfish creature just like you… except this creature leaves the toilet seat up. Only Jesus can be everything to you. He is pure and always good. He loves you unconditionally. He will always be there for you. Guys can be good to have around, but we cannot be Jesus for you.

It is good to want to be in a relationship, and one day the right guy will come along. Don't settle for any jerk that treats you like trash just because it's nice to have someone around. You deserve better. You deserve God's best.

Before we go on, let me talk to my brothers for a moment.

## A Few Words for the Guys

I'm a guy and I've hung around guys long enough to know that we really like women. Guys will do all sorts of stuff they do not really want to do simply because it might get the attention of women. Hair gel is a fitting example. I'm convinced that guys put products in their hair only because of girls. If you are ever around a bunch of guys and no girls are around, nobody will bother putting anything in their hair. Attracting women is also why we practise guitar, embellish about our mediocre sport careers, work on biceps at the gym, laugh loudly in public, put on cologne, wear nice clothes, and make fools of ourselves in public... It is all an effort to attract women.

We love the thrill of meeting women and exploring who they are. We love the thrill of the chase, and the chance to discover something foreign. We work hard at this and devote many hours to making our product more marketable to women.

This is why, once a guy has found a girl and has her locked in with a ring, he relaxes a little. Usually that means gaining weight. It seems like it's just part of the deal. In pursuit of the woman, the man works hard. He has had months or even years of being on his best behaviour, keeping up a standard of athleticism, opening doors, getting the right car, keeping it clean, buying her the right stuff, and paying for dates. After all that work, what guy couldn't use a rest for a few years?[44] Plus, there are the many gas exhalations which were suppressed during the whole dating process that now need to be released. This is all part of the deal.

---

[44] The only other person in a man's life who can get him back to a routine of sweating and eating properly is his doctor.

Though pursuing women comes naturally to guys, we don't always pursue women for the right reasons. There is something unhealthy about a man's pursuit of a woman when he has bought into the lie that he needs to have a girl on his arm to be seen as important—as justified—as a man.

Gentlemen, as a guy myself, I'm familiar with the struggle to understand whether or not you have what it takes to be a man. The two deepest questions a man asks himself are, "Am I man enough?" and "Do I have what it takes?" Whether you agree with these premises or not, you have to admit that they are in the top three, and follow only, "What's for dinner?"

No matter where I go I see guys trying to get other people to answer these "man enough" questions for them. It's like we are all walking around with a big question mark over our heads. The hope is that people will answer it for us. The problem is that they cannot. Society only seems to make the question marks bigger. Men seek to find validation in what we could call the *Big Three*: Money, Power and Women. If you can get any of the Big Three, or better yet, all of them, then our culture says, "You're a man now." If this were true, one would think that upon acquisition of any of the Big Three, a guy would have the "Am I man enough?" question answered and move on. But guys do not move on. The more sex a guy has, the more the question demands "Am I Man Enough". This leads him to search only for more. The question is never really answered by sex, money or power. It just gets louder for him.[45]

Men who look to women to answer their "Man Enough" question will never find the answer. That's God's job. A man should come to a relationship with a girl, not to find his answers in her, but to give his masculinity to her. God made us men to come into a relationship with girls from a position of strength— *not* for validation.

Until you can grasp that, guys, you are not ready to be a leader in a relationship, or in a family.

Just as guys do not want to be seen as the answer to all a girl's needs, girls don't want to be possessions or trophies, or have to validate their man every couple of hours like a parking ticket.

---

[45] Lookadoo, J. *The Dateable Rules*. (Hungry Planet, 2004) P. 20.

## Some Advice For All

We live with this tension: we were made for relationships but will often get into them for horrible reasons. Perhaps before we can experience the fullness of God's original plan, there is something deeper that needs to be dealt with in our own hearts so that we can fully give ourselves to another.

This is why I am proposing that you have the courage to devote a few years of your young life to being single. When you don't have to spend all your moments getting to know the person beside you, you can take some time to get to know yourself first. I challenge you to carve out some time to take a good hard look at who you are inside. Explore the dark places of your heart, the lonely places; revisit some of the tragedies and events that have shaped you thus far so that you can eventually come to the person you will marry with a sense of wholeness, not dependency. Tim Keller warns us, "While your character flaws may have created mild problems for other people, they will create major problems for your spouse and your marriage."[46]

## Getting the Most Out of Your Single Years

### 1. Learn to stand before someone leans on you.

You have to know who you are before you can offer anything to another person. Otherwise, you will seek them for your own identity. Again, people cannot fill the void that only God was meant to fill. Genesis 1:27 states that human beings are created in God's image. That means that we all have great value that comes from God — a value that no one can take away from or add to. If you are a human, you have great worth.

"But I don't feel like I'm worth anything."

It doesn't matter how you feel. Feelings don't change the truth. I may feel like the water in the ocean is not wet, but that doesn't change the fact that if I jump in, I'm going to get soaked.

---

[46] Keller, T. & K. *The Meaning Of Marriage: Facing the Complexities of Commitment with the Wisdom of God.* (New York, NY : Penguin Group, 2011).

St. Augustine said, "If, thinking of your frailty, you hold yourself cheap, value yourself by the price that was paid for you." This fourth century saint said that in order to see how valuable we are to Jesus, we need only look at what he paid for us on the cross. If we are that valuable to the King of kings, then we can be assured that we are valuable. When you understand that your value comes from God, and not your relationship status:

- You will not look to your spouse to meet all your needs.
- You will be a giver of the life that God gives you.
- You won't need to have a girl or a guy around to feel like you are a whole person.
- You can know there is a joy to be experienced even when you feel like you are "the only one without a date" on Friday night.
- You can attend someone's wedding and not spend the whole day pouting that it's not yours.
- You can enjoy the gift of today.

Your identity should be primarily found in God. Until you accept this as truth and apply it to your life, you are not ready to be in a relationship. You will be a leech. Leeches suck the life from people — they do not give life.

## 2. Become the one that "your one" will want to be with.

Were you ever encouraged at camp or at youth group to participate in an exercise called "My Future Husband/Wife Wish List"? You know, the one where you list all the qualities you would like to see in your future mate. I'm not sure where I stand with making these lists. There are pros and cons to making "The Future Mate List." On the "cons" side, jotting down your "future spouse" seems a little bit like making a shopping list for a human being. This, to me, is just a little too much like our consumer-driven culture mixed with a brush of idealized romanticism. Thinking you can order the "Perfect Guy/Girl" is setting you up for disaster. I figure you might as well order a leprechaun while you're at it.

On the "pros" side, however, making this type of list does fit with the point I'd like to make in this section. For that reason, I will continue. You should have an idea of what characteristics you would like the person you will marry to have. We all have some sort of criteria in our head anyway. I don't see the harm in putting pen to paper in this matter.

However, I do add a caution to this process for it can quickly get out of control. We are not describing the person who will fulfill all our desires, help us reach a certain social status, or make all our dreams come true. As we've said before, this is not the purpose of marriage. Tim Keller cautions us against this kind of thinking:

> Both men and women today see marriage not as a way of creating character and community but as a way to reach personal life goals. They are looking for a marriage partner who will 'fulfill their emotional, sexual, and spiritual desires.' And that creates an extreme idealism that in turn leads to a deep pessimism that you will ever find the right person to marry.[47]

Nevertheless, I do recommend jotting down some characteristics because, as you think and pray about what you are looking for in a spouse, the next plan of action is to *make sure that you become the type of person he or she is going to want to spend time with…* a lot of time. I will once again address the guys, but it applies for both genders.

Gentlemen, do you want to marry a girl who understands the world and can have an educated conversation with you? If you want someone with a brain, you'd better make sure you get your nose in a book, go to school, and follow current events.

Do you want a girl who is athletic and in good shape? You had best start doing some sit-ups now because, chances are, she's going to want to be with someone who is in shape as well. ("Round" doesn't count as a shape in this case.)

Do you want to marry a girl who doesn't have a history of sleeping around? Then don't go sleeping around, because, chances are, she's going to want to marry someone who has sexually saved himself for marriage. This means setting clear boundaries about how far you will go physically with the person you are dating. Treat her as you would want someone

---

[47] Keller, T. & K. *The Meaning Of Marriage: Facing the Complexities of Commitment with the Wisdom of God.* (New York, NY : Penguin Group, 2011). p. 25-26.

treating your future wife. Do not treat any girl you date physically like a spouse until she actually is your spouse.

My last example is the most important. Guys, do you want to marry a girl who is in love with Jesus? Trust me, you want Jesus to be her first love. If Jesus is her first love, this means that shopping, partying, reading trashy romance novels, and trying to get you to fulfill all her needs will not get top priority in her life. Loving Jesus will ensure that all her other loves are kept in check. In order to land a girl like this, you'd better get down on your knees and bury your nose in a Bible. Guys like that are the sort of men that quality girls tend to seek.

Though opposites may attract when it comes to personality, they seldom attract when it comes to character. For example, the star football player may by chance fall in love with the band's lead clarinet player, or the honours student may end up with a rocker. These are attractions that are based on opposite personalities and will often make for good high school movies. When it comes to character, however, you just do not see opposites attracting.

Here is my argument simplified: Do you want to find a good girl? Become a good guy.

## 3. Commit to character development.

You are going to need character to build a strong marriage. Character isn't something that you get overnight. Santa doesn't put it under the tree, and it isn't available to download. You gain character by making right decisions over a period of time. Seek to do the right thing even when it is difficult and when no one is watching.

Character is also built by enduring difficult seasons in life and remaining true to your convictions, your faith in God, and your unswerving trust that he is always good. You grow in character when you turn to God, not to drugs, alcohol, relationships, sex, pornography, or anything else that would ask you to compromise your integrity and character.

Our character is what sets the path for the types of decisions we will make in life. "A man's character determines his destiny." That was my favourite line from the 2002 Kevin Kline movie, *The Emperor's Club*. Paul talks about this concept of "reaping what you sow" in his letter to the Galatian church:

> Do not be deceived. God cannot be mocked. A man reaps what he sows. The one who sows to please his sinful nature, from that nature will reap destruction; the one who sows to please the Spirit, from the Spirit will reap eternal life. (Gal. 6:7-8)

Ever wonder what makes a bitter old man/woman so bitter? He or she has chosen to be cynical over the course of his or her life, seeing the world with glass-half-empty goggles, and planting thoughts of hopelessness and despair day after day, year after year. My grandma, the most joy-filled, godly woman I know, got that way because she planted trust, faith, and hope throughout her life. She is a beautiful lady today because she chose to live in this light rather than dwell in the darkness.

I turn again to C.S. Lewis for his timeless wisdom on this subject.

> Every time you make a choice you are turning the central part of you, the part of you that chooses, into something a little different from what it was before. And taking your life as a whole, with all your innumerable choices, all your life long you are slowly turning this central thing either into a heavenly creature or into a hellish creature; either a creature that is in harmony with God and with other creatures, and with itself, or else into one that is in a state of war and hatred with God… each of us at one moment is progressing to one side or the other.[48]

What kind of person are you becoming? I hope you see that this chapter is about much more than just relationships. It is about the type of person you are becoming. Once the trajectory is set, God can bring the right person into your path and walk with you as you pursue Jesus together.

## When the Time Is Right

That desire you have to be married, or just in a relationship one day, is a good thing. It is God's wonderful gift to bring men and women together to complement each other, and to worship God as two people joined

---

[48] Lewis, C.S. *Mere Christianity*, (HarperCollins, New York, NY., 1952). P. 92.

together as one. Marriage, done God's way is a beautiful thing. Keller writes,

> To be loved but not known is comforting but superficial. To be known and not loved is our greatest fear. But to be fully known and truly loved is, well, a lot like being loved by God. It is what we need more than anything. It liberates us from pretense, humbles us out of our self-righteousness, and fortifies us for any difficulty life can throw at us.[49]

Until that day, when God leads you to the person he has prepared for you, commit these next years to the process of building character. Do not become a leech — be a giver. Find out who you are and what God wants you to contribute to this world. Then you will be the one prepared to meet someone else. May God bless you one day with a great marriage that honours his great plan, from Adam and Eve to the great wedding when Jesus comes back to marry his church.

## Recommended Resources About Marriage:

Keller, Tim and Kathy. *The Meaning of Marriage: Facing the Complexities of Commitment with the Wisdom of God.* (New York, NY: Penguin Group, 2011).

Tripp, Paul. *What Did You Expect?: Redeeming the Realities of Marriage.* (Wheaton, Ill: Crossway Books, 2010).

Eggerichs, Emerson. *Love & Respect: The Love She Most Desires; The Respect He Desperately Needs.* (Nashville, Tenn.: Thomas Nelson, 2004).

Harvey, Paul. *When Sinners Say "I Do": Discovering the Power of the Gospel for Marriage.* (Wheaton, Ill: Crossway Books, 2010).

---

[49] Keller, *Meaning*, p92

# LIFE HACK #8
# EMBRACE THE DESERT

At my high school graduation ceremony, the class valedictorian read to us from Dr. Seuss' book, *Oh, The Places You'll Go!*[50] I admit that I'm a big Doctor Seuss fan so I remember the moment well. This book was the perfect choice for such an occasion. Inspiring and smile provoking, the story stirs up excitement and wonder about the life that lies ahead for every grad.

There is one part to Seuss's story, however, that is not so positive or inspiring. It is actually a little discouraging; a part we would all like to skip over. It reads like this:

> Wherever you fly, you'll be best of the best.
> Wherever you go, you will top all the rest.
> Except when you don't.
> Because, sometimes, you won't.
> I'm sorry to say so but, sadly, it's true

---

[50] Geisler, Theodor. *Oh, The Places You'll Go!* (Random House, 1990)

> That bang-ups and hang-ups can happen to you.
> You can get all hung up in a prickle-ly perch.
> And your gang will fly on.
> You'll be left in a Lurch.
> You'll come down from the Lurch with an unpleasant bump.
> And the chances are, then, that you'll be in a Slump.
> And when you're in a Slump, you're not in for much fun.
> Un-slumping yourself is not easily done.

What's all this about hang-ups and prickly perches, lurches and slumps? Is that really appropriate for all the pomp and pageantry that goes into a graduation ceremony? Graduation is supposed to be positive, but here the usually charming Dr. Seuss has suddenly turned into Dr. Downer, spoiling everything with all this negative talk!

And he calls himself a *doctor*?

I guess Seuss is the one honest enough to alert us, with or without a rhyme scheme, that one day our rump could hit a bump and all of a sudden we'll be in a slump.

The point Seuss is making is that times of difficulty happen to everyone in some way or form; it's natural; it's part of life. Just as we must all breathe oxygen and eat food to live, we all suffer. This chapter's Life Hack is learning to embrace the reality of suffering with joy.

This is what the Bible offers us: "Consider it pure joy *when* you face trials of many kinds" (James 1:2). Telling someone to suffer with joy sounds as counter-intuitive as telling someone to mourn at a wedding or dance at a funeral.

## *When* You Face Trials?

Here's the tough reality for us all. At some point we all hit some rough patches on our journey. The rough patches are different for everyone. Someone might get sick or have to deal with an unexpected death. It may be a broken relationship in the family, between friends or a romance gone wrong. Your trial may be a shattered dream you have always hoped would come true, or a time of loneliness or depression, a financial crisis, or something else that hits you out of the blue.

This chapter doesn't sound very inspiring does it? At least be grateful that I'm telling you the truth. Hallmark cards may sound better but will they help you with the challenges of the reality of adult life? I would love to tell you that once you graduate you will live happily ever after for the rest of your life. Happily ever after is for fairy tales and romantic comedies. The reality is that we are broken people living in a broken world.

## Why Does this Have to Happen?

Why is there so much suffering and evil in the world? This is the question I have asked and, as a pastor to the whole spectrum of ages, I get asked the most. While I do not claim to understand everything that God does, I know that God always has a purpose. We are told that the God of the Bible, "works all things according to the counsel of his will" (Eph. 1:11). Your life and everything that happens in it fits within that "all things" within his will. I have learned that while we don't always know the why of what God is doing, Christianity speaks the strongest of any worldview in assuring us that there is a why for what we are going through. This chapter will focus on just one aspect of why God allows suffering: he wants to teach us something through it. I am aware that there are many other explanations and reasons that could be covered on this important topic. Here in this chapter, we do not have time to cover them all.

## When God Uses Suffering to Teach Us Something

I have the data that comes from looking back at what kinds of events God has used to shape me into the person I am today. I wish I could say I had learned the best lessons on the sunny summer days when I felt healthy, energized and found a twenty-dollar bill in the pocket of an old pair of shorts. While I love those days, looking back, it wasn't those days when I learned the most. It was the opposite.

The tough days, the dark days, the confusing days were the days when I learned the most.

I think of my formative years between eighteen and twenty, when my hockey "career" was the arena where God taught me the most powerful lessons. Growing up as a typical Canadian, I had wanted so badly to be a professional hockey player. A goalie, I wanted to be a star, make amazing saves and single-handedly win games for my teams... all the way to the Stanley Cup.

Instead of being a star, I sat on the bench as a backup goalie. My job was to open the gate and watch my teammates live out their dreams and get scholarships. That was painful. Looking back, I realize it was the best thing for my ego. God was doing something in my heart during those years. He was hard at work breaking that which needed to be broken, softening that which needed to be softened, and molding that which needed to be molded.

These are the kinds of things that God does when he wants to shape your character. I could give countless more examples.

C.S. Lewis wrote, "God whispers to us in our pleasures, speaks in our conscience, but shouts in our pain. Pain is God's megaphone to rouse a deaf world."[51] Today I can see how God has used pain to change my heart, desires, values, and the way I interact with people. I have learned to be less shallow, selfish and proud; and more gracious, kind and thoughtful – all in the classroom of pain. As he has done with me, so he may do with you.

God will bring pain into our lives to bring attention to an area he wants to refine. It will hurt, but we are always better off after going through it. Surgery is never fun while you're being cut open with a knife. But the surgeon is a trained expert and when he operates he is making you a stronger, healthier human being. God cuts us open and, although it hurts, it is always for our good. When you're under the knife of the Almighty Surgeon, remember that it's not that God has abandoned you or that he is not good. It is, in fact, quite the opposite.

## When God Wants a Man

When God takes you through a harsh period in your life, he is leading you somewhere you wouldn't be able to get to without first going through the painful trial. I include this lengthy poem to illustrate how God shapes a person that he has called to do great things. I have had to shorten parts of

---

[51] Lewis, C.S. *The Problem Of Pain.* (New York, NY.: HarperCollins, 1940).

it for the sake of space. While the author is the unknown, the message is clear.

> When God wants to drill a man and thrill a man and skill a man
> When God wants to mould a man to play the noblest part;
> When he yearns with all his heart to create so great and bold a man
> That all the world shall praise,
> Watch his methods, watch his ways!
>
> How he ruthlessly perfects whom he royally elects;
> how he hammers and hurts him,
> And with mighty blows coverts him
> How often he disappoints whom he sacredly anoints!
> With what wisdom he will hide him;
> never minding what betide him
> Makes him lonely so that only God's high messages shall reach him
> So that he may surely teach him
> what his heavenly Father planned.
>
> Then to test his Spirit's wrath,
> He throws a mountain in his path,
> Puts a bitter choice before him
> and relentlessly stands o'er him
> Climb or perish, so He says
> But watch His purpose, watch His ways!
>
> When his feet are torn and bleeding;
> yet his Spirit mounts unheeding
> Blazing newer paths and finds;
> Lo, the crisis, lo, the shouts that would call the leader out
> When the people need salvation does he rise to lead the nation;
> Then does God show his plan
> And the world has found its man.

Put so eloquently, that's the kind of process I am talking about. Let's look at a biblical case study that once again shows how God uses suffering to teach us what we need to learn in order to become the people he wants us to be.

Life Hacks

# How Moses Got a New Heart

Moses is an Old Testament case study we can look at to see how God uses suffering to break a person in order to shape them for greater purposes. It is good to know the stories of these Old Testament guys because one day you are going to run into them in Heaven and it will be awkward if you know nothing about what they did or why they were in the Bible.

Moses' story is found in the book of Exodus. It was a time when the Israelites were in Egypt, forced to work making bricks all day. Moses spent his early years in Pharaoh's house being told that he was a somebody. He was important, rich, and an adopted member of the Egyptian royal family. Unlike the other Egyptians born in nobility, Moses also had another side to him. He was a Hebrew man living in a country where Hebrews worked as slaves. One day Moses witnessed an Egyptian man beating a Hebrew slave, and he went to stop the injustice against a fellow Jew. Moses stepped in and, in the process, killed the Egyptian.

Word soon got out that the Prince of Egypt was now a murderer. A warrant went out for the young Hebrew's arrest. If Moses had been caught, he would have been punished by death upon the order of Pharaoh. Moses was forced to flee for his life, out of Egypt and into the wilderness of Midian.

You might not know much about Midian. Let me help you out a bit. It was a desert region. The average temperature there was forty-eight degrees Celsius in the summer. Moses worked there for forty years as a shepherd. Herding sheep was one of the lowest occupations on the social scale. Shepherds did not own land. They did not even own their sheep. In the desert, there were no storehouses of grain. You didn't know where you would find water. There was no protection from wild animals or robbers.

Moses, the man who once dined with princes, now lived with sheep in the desert.

His beard grew long, his clothes got dirty and he just chased sheep around. It was hardly the luxurious life of his younger days in Egypt. But living in the wild became a training ground for Moses. It was here that

God did a deep work in the heart of his soon-to-be great leader. It was in this difficult time that a broken Moses was rebuilt.

The good news is that God had a lot of room in this place to do his work in his leader. In the desert, there were few distractions from other people, the business of the city, or Egyptian culture. There was no cell reception or WiFi. It was just really quiet. Moses was going to learn to hear God's voice in the quiet. His God was going to teach him some things.

After forty years in the desert, Moses woke up one day and his season of training was over. God was ready to use him. While he was walking on a mountain God spoke to Moses in a burning bush. Moses removed his shoes as a sign of humble submission. A different man emerged from that desert. God was ready to present Moses with a new mission:

"Go and deliver my people from Egyptian captivity."

Moses responds, "Who am I that I should go to Pharaoh and bring the Israelites out of Egypt?" (Ex. 3:11). The between-the-lines translation of this statement is: "God, I'm nothing."

Moses clearly doesn't think he is the right guy for the job anymore. This shows some interesting insight into how God prepares people before he uses them for great things.

Before God can use you, he needs to break you. Charles Spurgeon, the great 19th century English preacher (and a man familiar with debilitating illnesses), declared, "The Lord gets his best soldiers out of the highlands of affliction." It is those who have persevered through valleys of difficulty that become God's best warriors. Great wine got that way because some grapes were squished and then left to sit for a while.

Remember when Moses thought *he* could be the one to deliver the Israelites from Egyptian slavery? He thought he could do it all himself, by his own might. God needed to break that independent part of Moses so he could learn total dependence on God.

It was through pain and difficulty that Moses and all God's leaders have learned this truth: We really are all a bunch of nobodies. The good news is that God is in the business of using nobodies to accomplish his work. But not just any nobodies— the one's that *know* that they are nobodies.

What Moses learned by hanging out with sheep is what I learned sitting on a junior hockey bench. For us proud, sinful humans, embracing our nobody-ness doesn't come naturally — it comes with suffering. Paul says,

> Brothers, think of what you were when you were called. Not many of you were wise by human standards; not many were influential; not many were of noble birth. But God chose the foolish things of the world to shame the wise; God chose the weak things of the world to shame the strong. He chose the lowly things of this world and the despised things and the things that are not, to nullify the things that are, so that no one may boast before him. (1 Cor. 1:26-29)

God takes his servants down to nothing so they will realize that their lives are not about them, their talents, or their accomplishments. Their lives are reserved for God's glory. God says to Isaiah, "I will not share my glory with anyone else" (Is. 42:8). He does not want people to take the credit for the things that he does. We could never handle that kind of glory anyway.

## Inspiration from Some Other Heroes

We appreciate the ability to overcome pain in order to create the strength and character that we see in the lives of Bible characters like Abraham, Jacob, Joseph, Moses, David, Ruth, Mary, Paul, Peter and others. We also find this theme in the lives of our favourite comic book characters.

Take Spiderman for instance. Peter Parker became an orphan early in life and was raised by his elderly aunt and uncle. Parker, a teenager living in New York City, grows up being bullied, and struggles with rejection, depression and loneliness. He gets a mean radioactive spider bite one day and discovers it has given him superpowers. It is Peter Parker's character, shaped by years of painful circumstances, that makes him the down-to-earth superhero people connect with and love. Rather than becoming one of the bad guys who have similar powers but lack the character, Parker uses his powers to help people and to stop crime. We admire his determination to rise above his circumstances. That is why the Spiderman story has connected so powerfully with fans.

Another inspiring story of a courageous superhero overcoming early adversity is another famous *DC Comic* character. After witnessing his own parents' murder in cold blood, Bruce Wayne grows up in Gotham City with a thirst for justice. He commits to a life of training himself both intellectually and physically. He dons a bat costume and spends the rest of his life fighting crime as the legendary, Batman.

One more figure to mention is the iconic hero, Superman. To prevent his child's certain destruction on his home planet Krypton, a desperate scientist named Jor-El sends his newborn baby into space on a ship, in hopes that he might be able to grow up on another planet. The ship lands on Earth and is discovered by a farming couple who adopt the baby and raise him as Clark Kent. The orphaned Kent grows up with a passion for helping people, despite his notoriously crippling, allergic reaction to Kryptonite.

The creators of these three superheroes are telling us something about what makes a person great. There is something powerful in a story about a person who overcomes and uses difficulty early in his life to either strengthen his character or to redeem the injustice committed against him. As a result, this survivor of great tragedy becomes committed to a life of rescuing others from pain. He becomes, in a sense, a wounded healer.

Here's a question for you to consider: *If you had the power to be invisible, what would you do with it?* Would you use it for good or for evil? I believe it depends on your character. Romans 5:3-4 instructs us that our character is shaped by our suffering. The bad times can serve to make us better people. Or they can make us bitter. We get to choose which.

Do you want to do great things for God? If so, do not be surprised to find a direct correlation between the amount of holy ambition you have and the amount of suffering you go through. As one increases, it seems, so does the other. Remember that even fictitious places like Gotham City are better because of it.

## He Always Cares

When we go through difficult times, it is comforting to know we are not alone. Jesus himself knew what it meant to question the goodness of God in times of difficulty. His prayer in the Garden of Gethsemane shows that, though he is God, he too struggled with the fact that he would have to go through suffering. The night before the most agonizing day any human being would ever have to live through, on the eve of his crucifixion, Jesus prayed, "My Father, if it is possible, may this cup be taken from me. Yet not as I will but as you will" (Matt. 26:42).

To paraphrase, Jesus was saying, "God, I don't know what is going on right now. I know what I want to happen but I don't think it is going to go my way here. I know that you know what is best and so I surrender to whatever you want."

We do not always understand why we have to go through the difficulties we face, but we do know that we will never suffer alone.

Jesus is a God who knows suffering. He comes near and suffers alongside us. While he walked on earth, Jesus experienced the same kind of trials we go through. There is a Greek word used twice in the New Testament, *splankzinomai*, meaning a "deep, gut wrenching grief." At the death of Lazarus in John 11, Jesus felt splankzinomai over the death of his friend. Our God knows the deep grief one feels when mourning the loss of a loved one.

He knows other forms of pain too. He was betrayed by a close friend; he knew anger and experienced disappointment. Jesus was often misunderstood and faced constant persecution that ultimately included his own death. Isaiah calls him, "a man of sorrows, familiar with suffering" (Is. 53:2). This is the beauty and intimacy that the Christian God offers. He is a God who, as David says, "is close to the brokenhearted" (Ps. 34:18) because he knows how much we need a God who says, "Me too."

Of course you may not feel as if God is close. He may even seem very distant in the middle of difficult situations. In pain, our emotions love to take over and cause us to think and act irrationally. Our emotions may tell us that God is not good, that he doesn't actually care about us: or perhaps that he has abandoned us altogether. These feelings are not a reflection of truth, however true they may feel at the moment. Jesus promised, "I am with you always" (Matt. 28:18).

When I was in elementary school, one of the most popular book series was the *Where's Waldo* collection. On each page of the books the author hides a candy-cane-stripe-shirted character named Waldo that readers have to find amidst a frenzy of activity. I spent months of my life searching for this guy. The pattern became predictable. In the early pages of every book, Waldo was easy to find. As you got further into the book, Waldo was more hidden. You always knew he was there: you just did not always know where. We all trusted the author, but sometimes it took a little more work to find him.

Sometimes in our lives it is obvious that Jesus is present and right there along with us. Other times it may seem like he is nowhere to be found, or that he is doing a good job of hiding. In these times, we must trust that the one who promised, "I will never leave you nor forsake you" (Deut. 31:6, Heb. 13:5) really meant it.

What is most true of God is what you believed when you were in your right mind — when you were thinking clearly before you got all worked up and emotional. It is funny how we can be so quick to give up on God and throw away our faith in him when we are feeling the least rational. Suffering has a way of doing this to even the strongest of saints. If you find your feelings taking over with lies about God's character, fight to keep perspective. Trust that God is who he says he is, regardless of how you may be feeling.

God is always there. God is always good. It can be easy to lose sight of that when we are focusing on our circumstances.

## Living in the Tension of Genesis and Revelation

Though our world is broken, we also have this promise that one day everything is actually going to work out. Until then, we are caught between the fall of humanity in Genesis 3 and the culmination of history in Revelation 21.

We must develop a trust in God that is anchored in the truth that God is always good and that there will be a day when our hearts' true desires will finally reach their fulfillment. The gift of pain and disappointment is a reminder that this earth is not our home and that heaven's joys will come to all who endure. Our earthly difficulties call us to look elsewhere for hope, for another day ahead that is not yet here. There will be a day when there will be no more pain. There will be a day when our questions will be answered and our doubts satisfied. There will be a day when Jesus will wipe away every tear from our eyes. I am very excited for that day.

This expectation calls us to consider all our "light and momentary troubles" (2 Cor. 4:17) in light of the joy that awaits those who belong to Jesus. Revelation 21:1-4 gives us an even clearer perspective of the new life that awaits us in the new heaven and the new earth promised in Revelation:

> I heard a loud voice from the throne saying, "Behold, the dwelling place of God is with man. He will dwell with them, and they will be his people, and God himself will be with them as their God. He will wipe away every tear from their eyes, and death shall be no more, neither shall there be mourning, nor crying, nor pain anymore, for the former things have passed away."

C.S. Lewis describes this coming joy as he concludes the Narnia series. In *The Last Battle*, the characters step out of Narnia and into Aslan's country. Lewis describes the new world to come this way:

> The term is over: the holidays have begun. The dream is ended: this is the morning. And as he spoke, he no longer looked to them like a lion; but the things that began to happen after that were so great and beautiful that I cannot write them. And for us this is the end of all the stories, and we can most truly say that they all lived happily ever after. But for them it was only the beginning of the real story. All their life in this world and all their adventures in Narnia had only been the cover and the title page: now at last they were beginning Chapter One of the Great Story which no one on earth has read: which goes on forever: in which every chapter is better than the one before.[52]

---

[52] Lewis, C.S. *The Last Battle* (New York, NY.: HarperCollins, 1956).

When life disappoints us, we need heaven's perspective. Heaven's perspective tells us that our earthly life can be tough, but it is not permanent. All the trials and troubles will seem like one of those rainy, November recess breaks in the third grade. Difficult as they may have been, today I don't remember much about those recesses anymore. Let us remember, the aches and pains of life are daily reminders that we were not made for this world. We have a home awaiting us where we will live forever, where there will be no more disappointment, aches or pains.

Sometimes heaven feels like a long way off. I can understand that. In the meantime, I encourage you to hold on, to wait, to trust that God is always good and that he has this world under control. Your life will be full of good times and bad times. We all go through seasons of difficulty, pain, and disappointment, but no season lasts forever. Things happen throughout our lives that are horrible: accidents, pain, family issues, betrayal by friends. At the time it may feel as though it's the end of the world, the end of your life; as if there will be no end to the hurt, the pain, the difficulties. As adults, we can look back on our childhood traumas and see that they were only for short seasons; that there was life - good life - later. Not only that, adults can see that most of the things that troubled us as young people were not such big deals.

## What Do You Really Want?

Even though suffering helps us grow in character and gets us excited about heaven, I still hate it. To be honest, it still seems a little strange that the Bible would tell us to rejoice when we experience suffering. (See Romans 5:3-10 and James 1:2.) What I have learned is that my feelings about suffering tell me a lot less about the Bible and more about the condition of my own heart.

It seems strange that the Bible tells us to be thankful in suffering until we understand what the Holy Spirit working through the biblical writers is trying to tell us. I hope you will see that how you view suffering will be determined by what you value in life.

For instance, if your highest values are comfort, security and happiness (as is the case with the majority of us), everything that you do will be in an effort to be more comfortable, more secure and to increase personal happiness levels. This will be demonstrated by the people you hang out with, the job you have, the car you drive, how you spend your time, where you distribute your money, and even what you think about God. Notice that suffering — since it often makes you uncomfortable, takes away security and can result in unhappiness — must be avoided at all cost. This is why we have no idea why the Bible writers could unanimously agree that suffering is valuable and that we should be thankful for it.

Let's try a different approach. Let's say that Jesus is at the centre of your values. In everything you do, you want Jesus to be the most important thing to you. This means that you cry out like Paul in every area of your life, "I want to know Christ" (Phil. 3:10). You seek to know and follow Christ in your relationships, with your time, your finances, etc. The good news is that there is room for suffering in this. As we have learned in this chapter, it is often through our painful times that we learn the most about Christ. We learn lessons through suffering that we would never have learned if God had not brought it. This helps us to make sense of James 1:2 telling us to "count it all joy" when we face trials. Look at what Paul says in Philippians 3:10: "I want to know Christ—yes, to know the power of his resurrection and the *fellowship of sharing in his sufferings*, becoming like him in his death" (NIV, italics mine). Paul understood that knowing Jesus and living for him included suffering. Given these benefits, Paul was obviously cool with that.

Our personal values are revealed by how we approach suffering. Do you worship the gods of comfort, security and happiness? If so, you will forever be frustrated living in this broken and cursed world. The truth is that no matter what the commercials tell you, you will never be comfortable enough, secure enough or happy enough.

Do you worship Jesus instead of all those other things? He will take away your false hopes of comfort, security and happiness and will give you something much better.

## One Last Truth to Ponder

As this chapter closes, I have to put my pastor hat on for a moment. There is one last verse in the New Testament that has helped me so much on this sensitive topic. I think it will help you too.

Romans 8:29 says, "For those God foreknew he also predestined to be conformed to the image of his Son, that he might be the firstborn among many brothers and sisters." If this verse is true, it means that God has been at work before the beginning of time carrying out a plan for your life. That plan is about making you more like Jesus Christ. As we have learned in this chapter, becoming like Jesus does not come easy. It takes pain.

Living Romans 8:29 each day is the Life Hack that will brighten your interpretation of the events in your life. What is God doing bringing all these tough times in your life? He is doing it all to make you more like Jesus. When the circumstances and characters that come up in your life are interpreted through the Romans 8:29 filter, you have a paradigm for making sense of the pain. You may not like it but you can be assured that it is not a waste. That's why embracing these desert times in life are such an important life hack. I know that it has helped immensely to make sense of things, especially the pain.

For the character development of today, and the joys of heaven tomorrow, no matter what happens, you *can* know the secret of how to consider suffering pure joy.

Life Hacks

# LIFE HACK #9
# LOVE THE LOCAL CHURCH

I need to share an embarrassing story. It's near the end of the book now so I'm hoping you won't judge me too harshly.

I was once in a coffee shop with one of my best friends. We were engrossed in what we would call "a Man-Chat." It is only through assigning manly titles like "Man-Chat" that Christian guys justify the very unnatural behaviour of sitting in coffee shops and talking about their feelings with one another.

I am ashamed to say, on this day, our conversation got carried away. Even though we were both pastors, we were busy gossiping about one of our close, mutual friends. The conversation wasn't as much about him as it was about the girl he was engaged to marry. We did not like her. His fiancée was annoying to us. We went back and forth sharing the ways that she drove us crazy. We talked mostly about her character. We agreed that she didn't have any. She had a history of being flirtatious and unfaithful to him. We voiced our concern to each other about all of this, holding nothing back. Suffice it to say, we both felt our friend could do so much better and really should keep his distance from her.

As things spiralled out of control, my heart sank when I realized that our friend had in fact overheard the entire conversation! Needless to say, he did not appreciate the way we were talking about his beloved.

I am embarrassed to tell you that my friend's name is Jesus. His fiancée is the church.

This is not just some cute illustration. We easily slander that which Jesus loves most. In the Bible, the church is called Jesus' bride. He loves her and gave his life for her. All weddings here on earth are simply a preview of the greatest wedding that we anticipate. When God says it's time, Earth's time will be done and there will be one big wedding celebration. Jesus will be united to his church. It is laid out for us in Revelation 19:7-10:

> Let us rejoice and exult and give him the glory, for the marriage of the Lamb has come, and his Bride has made herself ready; it was granted her to clothe herself with fine linen, bright and pure"—for the fine linen is the righteous deeds of the saints. And the angel said to me, "Write this: Blessed are those who are invited to the marriage supper of the Lamb.

There will be a day when Jesus returns to marry his bride. Weddings worked a little differently in the Middle East back in the first century. After getting engaged to a girl, the future groom would return to his family's house in order to prepare an additional place that he and his bride would live in after the wedding. Jesus alluded to this when he said,

> In my Father's house are many rooms. If it were not so, would I have told you that I go to prepare a place for you? And if I go and prepare a place for you, I will come again and will take you to myself, that where I am you may be also. (John 14:2-4)

When the house was complete and set up with furniture, the father of the groom would give his son a head nod. It was then time to begin the wedding celebration.

When Jesus' Father gives the nod, it will be a wonderful day to call his rebellious, broken and beaten-up bride, the church, who will be clothed "with fine linen, bright and pure" (Rev. 19:8). If Jesus loves the church this much, we might pause and consider what kind of value we put on her as well.

## Why Church Is a Life Hack

"Love the church" is our final life hack because it provides each person on Earth the opportunity to be a part of something that is exhilarating, meaningful, eternal and much bigger than anything he or she could ever do on their own. Catch Jesus' vision for what a local church can be and you will never be bored for the rest of your life. Sadly, however, many churches lack Jesus' vision. So, before moving forward, we must address some of the baggage attached to the word "church."

## A Few Things To Clarify About Church

### 1. What is a Church?

When I am talking about church, I am not talking about buildings or institutions. During the Protestant Reformation of the 16th century, the Reformers made sure people got this part straight. They talked about how there were two kinds of church: the visible and the invisible. The visible church is the buildings, the hierarchies, the robes, the bells, the smells, and anybody who can either be seen in a church or associating with one. At the risk of being redundant, the visible church is anything associated with "church" that you can see with your eyes. The Reformers knew that not all who called themselves part of "the church" would actually be part of God's people. They needed a term that helped distinguish the counterfeit from the real.

Jesus warned us in advance that this would be a problem. He told us that many would come *in his name* who knew nothing about truly following him. He warned us that evildoers would show up wearing his jersey but really be playing for the wrong team. Jesus knew that enemies of the church would even rise up from within it. "Beware of false prophets, who come to you in sheep's clothing but inwardly are ravenous wolves" (Matt. 7:15). Jesus was also well aware that Satan planted weeds among the wheat (the true church). Jesus taught that it would not be until the last day that the Father would separate the weeds from the wheat (Matt. 13:30). Until then, the wheat and weeds are intermingled in every church. It is no surprise that false teachers and pesky, parasitical weeds have been a problem throughout church history. Jesus said it would happen.

The Reformers taught us that the invisible church is the true church— the true bride of Christ. This true church is made up of people who are saved by Jesus and lovingly follow him as his disciples. They are the multitudes of worshippers that will not be seen assembled all together until they gather in Heaven as promised in the book of Revelation. The Greek word, "church," is *ekklesia*, which means, "the called out ones". They are called out from the world and its pursuits, choosing instead to live for God alone. You cannot tell a Christian by their denomination, their clothes, their car, the size of their family, or their job. Being a Christian is a matter of the heart and, since we cannot see inside people's hearts with our eyes, the true church is called the invisible church. From now on when I refer to "the church" I will be talking about the invisible church, even though once in awhile I will refer to a church building. I'm confident you will be able to figure out the difference.

The church will go on forever. Nations, schools, businesses, dynasties, and trends will all come and go, blowing through history like wind. God made the world because he wanted a church. Today, Jesus is building that church.

In this last chapter I want to inspire you to consider getting excited about being a part of *the* church and *a* church and how you can join the most exciting, influential movement in world history.

## *2. Sometimes People Hurt Us*

Sometimes people's experience with the church is not so pleasant. Let's talk about what you should do when this happens.

As we get older, we gain experiences both positive and negative. That's part of life. If you're around church long enough, you will start to accumulate some negative experiences. You may start to see inconsistencies between the teachings of Jesus and the actual practices of the church and church people.

As you look around at different churches you may be sad to find that there is no such thing as a perfect church. If you study church history you will be hard pressed to find any perfect church.

What about the early church? This example proves my point well. Consider the sexual messes in Corinth that Paul had to confront. Consider the legalism that broke out in "foolish" Galatia (Gal. 3:1). Read the letters to the seven churches in the first three chapters of Revelation. False teaching, apathy, Satan worship— they had it all.

The reason churches are not perfect is that churches are full of people, and people are not perfect. The Christian worldview clearly teaches that everybody sins (Rom. 3:23). If a church has people in it, we should not be surprised to find that churches have sin in their midst. I know that there is sin in my church, because I am a sinner and they still let me keep coming back. If they let you through the doors, that's just one more sinner to add to the mix.

Knowing this, you now have a decision to make: how will you react when you see the problems created by the messy, sinful folks in *your* church?

## 3. How to Deal with Hypocrisy in the Church

I have empathy for those who struggle with the hypocritical behaviour of Christians. After all, if Christians are the people who supposedly have the truth, why don't they live like it? This question has been a constant struggle for me. A brief study of history reveals some ugly chapters in our story. Many terrible things were done in the name of Jesus that have made his name repulsive to the victims of hypocrisy and to those who have learned about it. But when the church fails (and it always will), God is consistently extending grace and love. God has never given up on his bride; therefore, neither should we.

I encounter people who offer their story about how they were hurt by the church. I should have asked what they meant because getting hurt by a church could mean falling into a baptism tank, having a cross-beam fall on their head, or burning their tongue on church coffee. What these folks actually mean is that they have had a bad experience with a person or group of people that have done them some harm.

Today, because I've seen it more, I counsel those who are hurt by some people to remember that those people don't represent the whole church or Christianity in general. If I have a bad experience with a math teacher, does that mean that all math teachers or math itself is corrupt? Rather than run away from God because someone has been hurt us, the best idea would be to run to God to find help and healing.

We must resist blaming all the "other people" for not doing their part in the church because, if we are honest, we are not doing ours very well either. Critiquing everyone else for the church's problems is like trying to beat up the air — it's tiring, it accomplishes nothing, and it just looks silly. There is a better way to deal with the problems in the church.

## How to Respond to Disappointment

Here is a painful yet important illustration for us. When I was a kid, there were times when I was hurt or did not get my own way. My go-to response was to throw a tantrum and let others know that I was very angry. I was great at throwing pity parties in my honour. This reaction is a common response among infants. Babies are quick to point out problems and cry about them. Often one baby will serve as a catalyst for another baby to cry, and as the crying babies multiply, a swell of awful noise reverberates around the room. When I became a man, I realized that crying and name-calling were not the best way to solve a problem. A man or woman of courage looks at a problem, puts their work boots on, rolls up their sleeves, and does everything they can to fix it.

Our churches are the family God has put us in. Any problems that come up are family problems. When we have family problems, we should not seek to swap our family in favour of a bigger, trendier, wealthier or more organized family. We grow up in the families that we are planted in. Of course, every family has that weird uncle. But we know that he is part of the family. You just learn to love your family and make the best of it.

God gives us the gift of community because we need each other. If you are going to grow as a follower of Jesus, you need to do so with a group of people who will help you out along the way. They need to be there to challenge you, pray for you, and mentor you; you can babysit their children and call them up when you need help moving a couch. A community that does church right is a gift to you and to your city. If you

# Love the Local Church

are not a part of a church community, it is like leaving a wrapped Christmas present just sitting there all year long. You are missing out.

Maybe your church is floundering a bit. God could use you to really turn things around. It has happened before. It can happen again. This is the story about the Meta-4s, an underachieving football team loaded with tremendous potential. This is how they got their game back.

For most football teams, the huddle is the place to discuss how to execute the next play. For the Meta-4s, the huddle was a fun place to hang out.

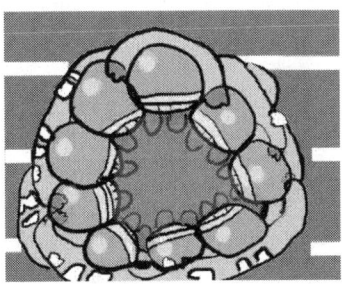

The team loved to huddle and never wanted to leave it. As a result, they never made any plays and never scored any points.

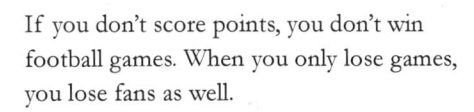

If you don't score points, you don't win football games. When you only lose games, you lose fans as well.

The team became very unpopular in the media. The Meta-4s became a joke in their community. What was their problem?

With the team's public image in shambles, the Meta-4s hired a consultant who gave the team a facelift. They designed some futuristic new jerseys for the team.

In the huddle they complimented each other on their new outfits. So impressed were they about their new look, they never broke out of the huddle.

A little discouraged, the consultant suggested they return to the past. The Meta-4s changed their style to a more vintage look. Some welcomed the change while others did not. There was arguing in the huddle. This led to long, drawn out huddle meetings that resulted in more penalties and still no wins.

Finally the Meta-4s fired the consultant and hired a pastor from the local church!

His church used to be too focused on huddling without going out and making plays. One day, the church began to strategize about how to help people and make a real impact in their community.

They thrived outside of their huddle by working together to clean up the city, helping homeless people, and drilling wells to give people in Africa clean water.

The pastor taught the Meta-4s to make plays that turned into touchdowns that turned into wins. The Meta-4s were, "The greatest comeback story since the local church!"

The Meta-4s remind me that there is always hope for any church. Every church can learn to break out of a huddle and be a part of a mission. It does not take a consultant to make the comeback; it takes a leader with a vision.

We already have the vision. We need people to see it. We need the leaders to live it.

## You Are the Light of the World

Jesus told us, "You are the light of the world. A city on a hill cannot be hidden" (Matt. 5:14). Just as a candle should not be lit and then covered, neither should a church be given light and then hide it. Jesus said the church is the light of the entire world. This must have sounded crazy for this small group gathered on a Galilean hilltop. Could these few pawns (compared to the great Roman Empire) really influence the world? This was a lofty vision.

The disciples were few but they got off to a great start. The church's big start is found in Acts 2. There was an explosion of power and service infused into the first century culture. The early church did as Jesus ordered and brought light to the Roman Empire and beyond. This church was good news for the world in those days. Let me give you a few examples.

If you were a Greco-Roman female in the first couple of centuries, the church was good news because Christians believed people of both genders were made in the image of God. As a result, both genders were equal in value and dignity before God. If you were poor in that day then you were thankful the church was there to share its resources. Regardless of the money you had, in the family of God, all were equal brothers or sisters. The Romans believed that it was a father's right to discard or kill a child if he desired. It was the church that taught that children were a gift from God and kept each precious life alive. Moreover, if you were sick with plague, you were thankful for the presence of the church. Christians were the ones who did not flee from the terminally ill but stayed to care for the sick and dying. They assured those who were dying of their God-given dignity. Many of the caregivers caught the plague in the process.[53] The church was good news back then and it grew by millions, turning the Roman Empire upside down in only four hundred years.

Dr. R.R. Palmer summarizes the dynamic change of thinking that the "light of the world" introduced to Greco-Roman life. Secular historians note how the growing church made a dramatic impact on the empire at the time:

---

[53] "2000 Years of Jesus" by Kenneth L. Woodward. Newsweek Magazine, March 29, 1999.

> It is impossible to exaggerate the importance of the coming of Christianity. It brought with it, for one thing, an altogether new sense of human life… Where the Greeks had identified the beautiful and the good, had thought ugliness to be bad, had shrunk from disease and imperfection and from everything misshapen, horrible, and repulsive, the Christian sought out the diseased, the crippled, the mutilated, to give them help. Love, for the ancient Greek, was never quite distinguished from Venus. For the Christians who held that God was love, it took on deep overtones of sacrifice and compassion.[54]

Though people did not always agree with everything the early Christians claimed, they always knew that having them around benefited them. As historian Rodney Stark writes,

> To cities filled with the homeless and impoverished, Christianity offered charity as well as hope. To cities filled with newcomers and strangers, Christianity offered an immediate basis for attachments. To cities filled with orphans and widows, Christianity provided a new and expanded sense of family. To cities torn by ethnic strife, Christianity provided a new basis for social solidarity… once Christianity did appear, its superior capacity for meeting these chronic problems soon became evident and played a major role in its ultimate triumph… For what Christianity brought was not simply an urban movement, but a *new culture*.[55]

This Christianity was the invisible church made of regular people who were used by God to visibly transform the Roman Empire.

It is regular people who are out there making a difference. Often they go unnoticed. Consider the usher at your local church. Whoever takes the time to thank these people? Every week they are needed to step up, stand up and collect the money during the offering. Without them, there would be no money collected which means no bills would get paid. For my

---

[54] Palmer, Robert. *History of the Modern World: Since 1815.* (Alfred A. Knopf Pbl., New York, NY, 2001).

[55] Rodney Stark, *The Rise Of Christianity: A Sociologist Reconsiders History* (Princeton, NJ: Princeton University Press, 1996). P. 161-162.

money, the usher is one of the unsung heroes of Sunday mornings. They are trained, but still human enough to make their share of mistakes.

Each week I notice harmony between the team as they systematically did their synchronized backwards usher walk. You know they talk about it before and perhaps even practice at home. Then again, there is always enough confusion during the offering when someone is screwing up. Sometimes they accidentally pass a second plate down your row, one from each side, resulting in the embarrassing crisscross.

I can always spot a fresh recruit on the usher team. I'm talking about the replacement usher who was probably tapped on the shoulder at the last minute to cover for someone who slept in. You can spot a rookie usher in certain situations that call for the calm and expertise that only the experienced usher can provide. How does he or she react when there is only one person sitting in a row? The new usher hasn't yet learned how to non-verbally communicate with the solitary person in the pew. Do they want you to pass them a plate? The veteran can ask this with only a raised eyebrow or a subtle waving of the plate. This makes the person in the pew know the plate is available without the usher feeling pushy. Growing up in church I could appreciate the seasoned veterans and the hard work they put in every Sunday morning.

Though I've never formally served as an usher, I realize that I too can sometimes play a role in the passing-of-the-plates process. You may have had to as well. There are times during the offering where a "mid-row" usher is needed. This is the role of the person who needs to stand up and walk the plate over because the gap between is too big. If you have been in church long enough, you have done your part in walking a plate or two over.

That's just ushering. We all have a part to play in some way.

## Who Will Change the World?

I know a lot of people who want to do great things with their lives. They are just not sure how or what or where to get involved. There is so much need and so little...us. John Mayer's song, *Waiting on the World to Change* expresses a frustration within most of us today,

> Me and all my friends; we're all misunderstood;
> They say we stand for nothing and there's no way we ever could.
> Now we see everything that's going wrong
> With the world and those who lead it.
> We just feel like we don't have the means
> To rise above and beat it.
> So we keep waiting; waiting on the world to change.

Mayer has observed a group of people in society that wants to do something important but lacks the means to do so. The world's problems are overwhelming: hunger, corruption, disease, dire poverty, lack of education, and sex-trafficking are many people's daily reality. And we are only scratching the surface.

Who will change the world? The *United Nations* has tried to make peace in our world but have never managed to prevent international leaders who insist on using violent aggression. Governments have made laws but they have never made two enemies love each other. Businesses have created economic growth but their money has never manufactured joy. Schools have trained minds and given degrees but they have not changed hearts. Social agencies take care of children and host community events but they cannot make a father stay faithful to his family.

Despite the increase in education, higher agricultural yields, a developing global economy and community development programs, our global problems still linger.

Despite all the tremendous work that these advances and Non-Governmental Organizations (NGOs) contribute, they are neglecting the root of the problem.

In my life I have travelled to every continent on God's *green* earth (I have yet to travel to either pole). I have learned that even though people around the world may look different, we are all still the same. Humans have the same basic needs no matter where they live: air, food, water, love, acceptance, hope, purpose, dignity, and grace. We all need the same things, and we all struggle with the same kind of things: selfishness, fear, guilt, cowardice, worry, and hate. The Bible calls these struggles "sin". There is no one culture that is solely responsible for sin, nor is there any culture immune to its effects. Sin is a global problem.

The only one large enough to take on the problem of sin is God himself. Jesus (who is God) says he is light and that his church bears that light to the world.

The miracle is that even though God is our only hope, he brings hope to the world through people. Jesus uses regular people known as his body, the church, to accomplish his plan for our world as he has been doing all through history. This is why the church is the hope of the world. The church, when mobilized, is the most dynamic force this world has ever seen. You don't hear that bit of information on the news all that much.

Consider this example of the church's ability to mobilize for a good cause. Following Hurricane Katrina in 2006, the relief effort on the Gulf Coast of the United States was enormous. The Red Cross reported that ninety percent of the meals served to those hit by the record setting hurricane were prepared and served by Southern Baptist churches. This means that the churches were able to respond to the crisis faster than the Red Cross or the United States Government. How is that possible? It's because the church is located everywhere and its potential to make a global impact is incalculable.[56]

## Thank God for the Church

"The local church is the hope of the world."[57] This Life Hack is that you can be a local part of this global hope. My dream is to see generation after generation returning to a vision of the church as Jesus sees it: a vision with love, grace and tremendous potential.

Matthew Parris, a UK foreign correspondent, award-winning author, and a self-professed atheist, once wrote an article shamelessly admitting how vital the presence of the church is in Africa alone. "I've become convinced of the enormous contribution that Christian evangelism makes in Africa," Parris noted. He describes the church's impact in Africa as,

---

[56] Again with the help from an article on www.rickwarren.com (Accessed March 17, 2009).

[57] A common refrain from Pastor Bill Hybels of Willow Creek Church in Chicago, Ill.

> ...sharply distinct from the work of secular NGOs, government projects and international aid efforts...Education and training alone will not do. In Africa, Christianity changes people's hearts. It brings a spiritual transformation. The rebirth is real. The change is good. I used to avoid this truth by applauding — as you can — the practical work of mission churches in Africa. It's a pity, I would say, that salvation is part of the package, but Christians black and white, working in Africa, do heal the sick, do teach people to read and write; and only the severest kind of secularist could see a mission hospital or school and say the world would be better without it.[58]

When people take the call of God seriously and serve as light in the world, skeptics like Matthew Parris take note.

Parris observed that the world needs the church. This UK atheist has not given up on Jesus' bride. Neither have I. Nor should you. You can live today as if Jesus really meant it when he stood on a Galilean hillside and declared to all of us, "You are the light of the world" (Matthew 5:14).

May even devout atheists like Matthew Parris see what God does through your church and in churches all over the world and have no other alternative but to conclude,

"Thank God for the church!"

---

[58] Parris, Matthew. "As An Atheist, I Truly Believe Africa Needs God." www.timesonline.co.uk/tol/comment/columnists/matthew_parris/article5400568.ece. Accessed December 13, 2008.

## CONCLUSION
# THE LIFE-LONG PROCESS OF LIFE HACKING

We could go on, but I need to stop here. I originally wrote this book as an introspective way to grapple with some of the important lessons I have learned since graduating high school. Each chapter was a point I wish I could go back and tell myself to get working on. The chapters morphed into a book of Life Hacks that will hopefully be useful to anyone (of any age) who reads it.

The Life Hacks in this book were written to help you. They are penned with love and soaked in prayer. It is my desire that you will now go on to apply these principles, that in doing so you will discover the life God has given you, and that you will experience that life to the full (John 10:10).

There has been much to work through in this book of Life Hacks. We have wrestled with deep philosophical questions of the mind and the heart. We have considered living for eternity and yet committing to thrive in the present. We have concerned ourselves with the direction our lives are going while being set free from the trap of worry that we might not get somewhere.

We have also closely examined our relationships such as friendships and marriage. If that was not enough to chew on, we looked at the sensitive topic of how God uses suffering in our lives. Finally, we talked about the importance of the local church and how you can be a part of this unstoppable force, the hope of the world.

That's a great deal of ground to cover in a little book. I hope what you have found to work through here will be a catalyst for a lifetime of discovering the depth and beauty of a life lived fully for Jesus Christ.

That's what Life Hacks are all about. They are about making sure you are glorifying God with your life by honouring him each day.

That's the thing about our lives. They are unravelled one day at a time. God seems to be in no rush to make us the kind of men and women he desires for us to be.

## One Last Bit of Encouragement

Change is difficult and it takes a long time—except on TV. Married life has introduced me to those popular home renovation shows. These are the shows that begin with a tour of an old home. It has decor and design that is long past its prime. A distressed and cash-strapped young couple needs to upgrade the place so they call on two well-groomed, well dressed guys who show up, talk through a plan and within ten minutes in TV world, they are ready to tear the place apart. In thirty minutes the house is fully renovated and looking brand new.

I have a friend who has a family member that works as a plumber on one of these TV renovation shows. He tells me that his show is a little… "showy." While we are led to believe the hosts are the ones doing the work, they're mostly actors. One of the hosts merely shows up in the middle of the work project with the film crew for an hour. After make-up, with the cameras rolling he moves a few things around, works a power tool for a couple minutes, puts it down, wipes his brow and then takes off.

From watching these shows, one might conclude that home renovations are quick and easy. If it only took thirty minutes on TV, how long could it take in reality? This is the kind of thought that went through my mind when we began to finish the basement in my own home. Many months of measuring, cutting, measuring again, re-cutting, painting, and re-painting later, I have a new appreciation for the process of *real* improvement. After a day of hanging drywall with me, my friend Gary summed his assessment of my talents for, "Well Jon, after working with you all day, I realized your true calling…"

Thinking he was going to gush a little about my surprising talent for handling the tools, I pressed for the end of his thought, "Oh really, Gary…what's my calling?"

"Pastor."

He was right. I'll stick to pastoring. I'll stick to helping people become who God wants them to be. Here's one last bit of pastoral counsel: When you get through a book like this, you might think that life hacking were a simple, quick and easy process (just read a book and you're done!)

However, as I learned from trying to do my own home renovations, change is not as easy as we are led to believe. The process of applying the Life Hacks you have learned about doesn't happen overnight.

As you seek to apply what you have learned, give yourself lots of time and grace to learn what being a follower of Jesus looks like. James 4:6 reminds us, "God always gives more grace."

When you really understand what that little verse means, it is the best hack of all.

Life Hacks

Made in the USA
Columbia, SC
08 April 2018